DEFENDING
THE
CONSTITUTION

Also by Alan Dershowitz

DEFENDING THE CONSTITUTION

ALAN DERSHOWITZ'S SENATE ARGUMENT AGAINST IMPEACHMENT

ALAN DERSHOWITZ

HOT BOOKS

Hot Books may be purchased in bulk at special discounts for sales promotion, corporate gifts, fund-raising, or educational purposes. Special editions can also be created to specifications. For details, contact the Special Sales Department, Skyhorse Publishing, 307 West 36th Street, 11th Floor, New York, NY 10018 or info@skyhorsepublishing.com.

Hot Books® and Skyhorse Publishing® are registered trademarks of Skyhorse Publishing, Inc.®, a Delaware corporation.

Visit our website at www.hotbookspress.com.

10 9 8 7 6 5 4 3 2 1

Library of Congress Cataloging-in-Publication Data is available on file.

ISBN: 978-1-5107-6180-3
eBook: 978-1-5107-6181-0

Cover design by Brian Peterson

Printed in the United States of America

To my wonderful wife Carolyn, whom I love dearly, and who has supported and loved me despite disagreeing with some of my positions and enduring some of the repercussions.

TABLE OF CONTENTS

INTRODUCTION:
PRESIDENT TRUMP ASKS ME TO JOIN HIS IMPEACHMENT LEGAL TEAM

I n the weeks leading up to the impeachment vote in the House of Representatives—a partisan vote whose outcome was predetermined by the large Democratic majority—members of the president's legal team reached out to me inquiring whether I would be willing to join them in arguing against his removal by the Senate. As a liberal Democrat who voted for Hillary Clinton, I

felt somewhat conflicted emotionally. I was also feeling pushback from family members, especially my wife, Carolyn, who wanted me to maintain my independence and nonpartisan neutrality. I told the president's lawyers that I would not join the legal team as a full-fledged member involved in tactical, strategic, or factual issues, but I would consider playing a limited role as a constitutional advocate—a role I've played in other cases. I would be defending the constitution and the presidency, rather than any particular individual. As one lawyer of President Andrew Johnson put it at his Senate removal trial: I came to the defense table not as a "partisan" or "sympathizer" but to "defend the Constitution." Or as another put it: "A

greater principle is at stake than the fate of any particular individual."

I decided that if I were to agree to accept the limited role of presenting a constitutional argument against the removal of President Trump, I would begin by quoting these distinguished 19th-century lawyers.

My wife pointed out—quite correctly— that no matter how limited my role might be, I would be seen as an advocate for President Trump, thus compromising my neutrality, rather than for the Constitution. I knew she was probably right, so I did not immediately agree to play any role in the Senate trial.

While my wife and I were considering the options, we were invited to join a friend and his family for Christmas Eve dinner. We were orig-

inally going to have dinner in Miami Beach—where we spend the winter—on the day after Christmas, but we had to change our plans and go to New York for a funeral right after the holiday, so we moved our dinner up. His family had planned their event at the Mar-a-Lago Hotel in Palm Beach—where they were long-time members—so we drove up there to join them. We sat at a far corner of the massive dining room and were finishing our appetizers when President Trump and his family entered the other side of the room, a considerable distance away. When we accepted the dinner invitation at Mar-a-Lago, we knew there was a possibility the president would be there, but we did not expect to meet him in such a large room with so many people. But, as fate would have it, when I got in the buffet

line for the main course, he got behind me. I was surprised that the president was on the line instead of being served at his table. We said hello and I politely offered him my empty plate, which he politely declined. Then he said, "So, are you going to be my lawyer in the Senate. Everyone wants the job, but you're my first choice." I told him that I was considering it, but that my wife was opposed to me doing it, and he replied, "Bring her over and let me talk to her."

I went back across the large hall and found Carolyn eating her main course at our table. "The President wants to talk to you."

"About that?" she replied.

"Yes, about that."

Carolyn and I walked across the room and approached the president at his table, where

he was finishing his meal. I told him we would wait until he finished, but he got up and started talking to Carolyn. He asked her why she was reluctant to have me become his lawyer. She told him that she wanted me to maintain my independence and neutrality. He said that he thought she had a good point, but that this was a historic event, and that it was important for me to make the constitutional arguments. The discussion went on for several minutes, and at the end, President Trump turned to Carolyn and said, "I know how much Alan loves you and how much you love him, and he ought to listen to what you have to say, so you should discuss it and do what's best for you."

"But," he continued, "I really would like Alan to do it, and I think it would really be good for

the country if you and Alan decide he should do it."

Over the next several days, Carolyn and I discussed what role, if any, I should play in the Senate removal trial. In the end, we agreed that I would write and deliver the main constitutional argument against impeaching any president based on vague and open-ended criteria, such as the ones charged against President Trump, namely "abuse of power" and "obstruction of Congress." I would make my argument to the Senate and then leave. My role would be announced as a constitutional advocate and not as a general member of the defense team. The defense team agreed to this formulation, as did

President Trump, and, most importantly, as did my wife.

I then got down to the hard work of preparing a constitutional argument that I knew would be rejected by the vast majority of academics, pundits, talking heads, editorial writers, and others. Mine would be very much a minority view, though I was convinced that if the "shoe were on the other foot"—if Hillary Clinton had been elected president and were being impeached on these questionable grounds—many of those who would be criticizing my arguments would be agreeing with them.

I spent the next several weeks immersed in dusty old leather-bound books from the 18th and 19th centuries. I read all the debates about the adoption of the impeachment

provisions of the Constitution, the Federalist
Papers, Blackstone's commentaries on the
law, the arguments in the 1868 impeachment
and removal trial of Andrew Johnson, and
the contemporary scholarship regarding the
criteria for impeachment. I concluded that the
Framers would not have accepted such vague
and open-ended criteria as those charged
against President Trump. James Madison, the
father of the Constitution, explicitly opposed
the criteria of "maladministration" as a ground
for impeachment. He feared that so vague and
open-ended a criterion would result in the
president serving at the pleasure of the Senate.
Other founding fathers who attended the
Constitutional Convention expressed similar
fears and limited the constitutional criteria for

impeachment to treason, bribery, and other high crimes and misdemeanors. The addition of the words "and misdemeanors" left some room for interpretation, but My research made it clear that the framers did not intend and would not have accepted such standardless criteria as abuse of power and obstruction of Congress.

During the impeachment and removal trial of President Bill Clinton back in 1998, I had been interviewed by Larry King. In that interview, I expressed the view that a technical crime was not required for impeachment. I had not researched that issue thoroughly at the time because it was not disputed that Clinton had been charged with a crime, namely perjury. The issue in the Clinton case was whether perjury about a private matter—Clinton's sex life—was a high

crime. I said it was a low crime and thus not subject to impeachment. In the King interview, I made an off-the-cuff comment that a technical crime was not required if the impeachment targets a person who "completely corrupts the office of the president, who abuses trust and who poses a great danger to our liberty."

At the time I made it, I was aware that the academic consensus was consistent with the view I then expressed, and so I simply went along with that consensus, without doing my own research about an issue that was not germane to the Clinton case.

In the Trump case, on the other hand, a critical issue was whether a crime was required for impeachment, because the articles of impeachment did not charge any crime. I began

to research that issue when Hillary Clinton was running and it looked like she would likely be our next president. Republican zealots were demanding that she be locked up and were threatening to impeach her on the day she was sworn in. I decided to write a book about why impeachment would not be justified based on the evidence against Hillary Clinton. The original title for my proposed book was *The Case Against Impeaching Hillary Clinton*. When Donald Trump was surprisingly elected, I decided to continue the project and write a book entitled *The Case Against Impeaching Trump*. In doing research for that book, I concluded that the views I expressed in 1998 were not entirely correct. My research convinced me that although a technical crime was not required,

as I had said back then, criminal-type behavior akin to treason and bribery was required. More importantly, it was clear that abuse of power or other vague criteria would not be consistent with the words of the Constitution or with the intentions of its Framers.

I wrote a series of articles and short books in which I argued for more stringent criteria for removing a duly elected president. Then, when I signed on to make the Senate argument, I closeted myself in my Miami Beach apartment and dove into those dusty old 18th- and 19th-century volumes which I had collected over time. I took out my pen and paper and began to draft.

A writer for *Esquire* magazine, Tom Chiarella, asked if he could watch me work for several hours so he could chronicle what

he called "this historic matter." With my wife's permission, I agreed. Here is how he described my work patterns.

> He sits with his back half-turned to the window of his eighth-floor apartment in Miami Beach, wearing a striped button-down shirt loosely tucked into khakis, warm socks. ...
>
> Alan Dershowitz sighs and stares into his lap, where he's got a legal pad cocked against his thigh. His glasses descend the bridge of his nose as he works, until he looks the part of a college professor, which he was for more than fifty years, unpanicked by deadline.
>
> On that legal pad: Notes, which

become sentences, which are accumulating into an argument against the impeachment of Donald J. Trump, which Dershowitz is scheduled to deliver to the United States Senate in just three days.

Dershowitz's wife, Carolyn, a retired neuropsychologist, has set up a workspace for him on their dining room table, where he has piled earlier drafts of his argument and his ...primary sources....

Also in the shuffle of papers: a program, one page, from the concert he and Carolyn attended two nights ago. The Cleveland Orchestra was in town, performing Prokofiev. Dershowitz had gotten bored after intermission and

during *Romeo and Juliet, Acts 3 and 4,* had pulled out a black pen and started making notes for his opening argument in the impeachment trial, right there in the Adrienne Arsht Center for the Performing Arts in Miami.

- "Texts"
- "Framers"
- "Federalist"
- "3 impeachments"
- "Academics"
- "Question: Should there have been an investigation of Biden's company?"
- "Direct Threat to withhold (authorized) funds"

He wrote these things in the dark-
ened concert hall, and they are a little
smudgy now. He was looking at them
again last night, with a football game
on, as he read through the Federalist Papers. Now the papers and the books and
the chicken-scratched concert program
surround him as he untangles a tiny Mr.
Goodbar from its wrapper.

Watching someone write can be dull
work. Even Dershowitz, the legend, the
Harvard Law School professor who has
become about as famous as a working
lawyer can become in this world.

The guy who says he voted for
Hillary and yet still, at eighty-one, is

the kind of guy Donald Trump wants
standing up for him on the floor of the
Senate...

Watching Dershowitz work, it's
like this: Ink wires itself onto the page,
in the wash of his gimpy scrawl. The
scratching pen is audible over the dim
sound of beach traffic from below. Note:
No keyboard. He doesn't own one, nor a
computer.

The pages practically pile themselves.

He writes in a single pass, using
black roller-tip pens, bought in bulk
plastic containers like the ones Twiz-
zlers come in at Costco. He must have
sixty pens. Always on a white legal pad,

one of a half-dozen spread across the glass tabletop. He double-spaces naturally on the pad, in cursive.

I notice after a few hours: He doesn't slave over the words. It really seems as if he's never chosen a word he didn't like just fine. He rarely doubles back on his own prose on the handwritten draft. He appears to think comfortably in full sentences.

But no, it's Alan at his table. Anything can happen....

So I ask, Are you all alone on this? Is there some group of academics, or lawyers, who are behind you on your interpretation of the Constitution? Is there a body of thinkers behind you?

Are you reinventing the interpretation of the Constitution?

Dershowitz shakes his head. "I have nobody. No," he says. "I don't try to foster a following."

Dershowitz retrieves the pages from the fax in his wife's office, which takes up the pantry of their apartment. He then sits in a leather recliner and calls Kelley. He does a read-back with her, with his phone volume turned up to "Old Man."

It seems odd, at first, this manner of work. He writes so quickly, fires it off to Kelley. And yet even his fastest writing is slower than most people's regular-speed typing. In his way, he is deliberate. Contemplative. Slow.

Dershowitz clarifies that he is a liberal, that he did not vote for Trump, that he has agreed to work only to protect the Constitution. He does not support Trump's policies. Not on women's rights. Not on gun control. Not on the environment. Not on climate change. And so forth. He points out that his wife and his family opposed him working with the president's defense team.

"He didn't change my mind," she says. "I just thought it was important that Alan remain impartial.

"But I will admit that he listened to me." In the end, Carolyn was not going to stand in the way of her husband's desire to defend the Constitution. . . .

Dershowitz's son calls to beg him not to go on CNN again. He's communicated this to Dershowitz twice already today.

"I know," Dershowitz says. "It's more than that, actually."

Why do it then? What good does it do you to appear as a guest on television news shows?

"Look, I have an enormous amount of respect and love for my son. And I listen to everything he tells me," Dershowitz says. "But in the end, I have to make my own decision."

Dershowitz has rethought the ending. He's reading it back to Maura, a part of the speech in which he refers to an

argument he made about *Bush* v. *Gore*: "'I ask the distinguished members of the Senate to consider that heuristic—'" Dershowitz pauses then. "My son's going to kill me for using the word *heuristic*. '... that heuristic test in evaluating the arguments you have heard in this distinguished chamber, in this historic chamber.'" He gets to the end of that paragraph and circles the word.

Then he tells Maura, "All right. I think it's done."

He's all alone down here, working the case, performing a task you'd think would have been assigned to a team of lawyers at a high-powered firm.

But no, it's Alan at his table. Anything can happen.

"Okay, want to listen to me for a couple of minutes?" Dershowitz says. "Do you have a cough drop, Carolyn?" She's on the bed, reading a novel and watching the whole event with some trepidation. She gets up and gives him one. She takes a long look at him before she sits back down. "I've got a whole bag ready for tomorrow," she says. "You need to drink water, too."

"Cough drops are more important," he says. She laughs a little.

"Okay," he says. "Ready?"

When he next speaks, his voice is suddenly full-throated. Dershowitz jumps to his feet, pads across the worn, loose, and lumpy carpet in this beige

chamber, egg-crated in cement who knows when. He raises his hand in an imaginary wave to John Roberts. "Mr. Chief Justice," he says. "Distinguished senators, House managers and attorneys, and fellow Americans. . . ." He's positively animated, a little electricity running through his bones. His voice is rich, and he's taking deep looks beyond the corners of the room, calling up the nation.

Chiarella captured quite perceptively my work style. After completing my draft, I went to the capitol for three days. On the first, I made my seventy-minute argument. On the second day, I went to the White House to participate in

the unveiling of the President's Mid-East Peace Plan. On the third day, I went back to the Senate floor and answered seven questions put to me by Senators about my argument. My argument and answers are in the coming chapters, followed by an op-ed responding to the media distortion of what I actually said.

Entering the Senate chamber to speak on a historical matter is an awesome experience. I had been on the floor of that chamber once before: representing a Democratic Senator, Alan Cranston, who was facing ethics charges.

The awesomeness quickly vanished as Congressmen Schiff and Nadler delivered their partisan speeches. They made the Senate sound like a political rally. Though I personally share many of their political views, I thought it inappropri-

ate to have to listen to them in an impeachment trial of the president of the United States.

I nervously listened to the speaker who preceded me. When my turn came, I brought my old dusty books and my draft to the lectern and delivered my argument.

DEFENDING
THE
CONSTITUTION

DEFENDING THE CONSTITUTION: MY SENATE ARGUMENT AGAINST IMPEACHMENT[1]

Introduction

Mr. Chief Justice, distinguished Senators, House Managers, attorneys, and fellow Americans. It is an honor to stand before you and to

---

1   To watch or listen to my argument as I delivered it, please scan this code, or visit https://www.youtube.com/watch?v=uqmhfyH09jM&-feature=youtu.be

present the constitutional arguments against the impeachment and removal of this president, and any future presidents, who may be charged with the unconstitutional grounds of "abuse of power" and "obstruction of Congress." I stand today as I stood in 1973 for the protection of the constitutional and procedural rights of Richard Nixon, whom I abhorred and whose impeachment I personally favored, and as I stood for the rights of Bill Clinton, whom I admired, and whose impeachment I strongly opposed. I stand against the misapplication of the constitutional criteria in *every* case and against *any* president, without regard to whether I support his or her party or policies. I would be making the same constitutional argument had Hillary Clinton—for whom I voted—been elected and a Repub-

lican House had voted to impeach her on these unconstitutional grounds.

I will argue that the constitutional terms "high crimes and misdemeanors" do not encompass the two articles charging "abuse of power" and "obstruction of Congress." In offering that argument, I stand in the footsteps and spirit of Justice Benjamin Curtis, who was "of counsel" to impeached President Andrew Johnson, and who explained to the Senate that "a greater principle was at stake than the fate of any particular president," and of William Evarts, a former Secretary of State, another of President Johnson's lawyers, who reportedly said that he had come to the defense table not as a "partisan" or "sympathizer," but to "defend the Constitution."

The Constitution provides that the Senate

has the sole power to try all impeachments. In exercising that power, the Senate must consider three issues in this case: The first is whether the evidence presented by the House Managers establishes, by the appropriate standard of proof—which I believe is beyond a reasonable doubt—that the factual allegations occurred. The second is whether those factual allegations, if proved, rise to the level of abuse of power and/or obstruction of Congress. Finally, the Senate must determine whether abuse of power and obstruction of Congress are constitutionally authorized criteria for impeachment. The first issue is largely factual, and I leave that to others. The second is a combination of traditional and constitutional law that I will briefly touch on. My focus will be on the third issue—whether

abuse of power and obstruction of Congress are constitutionally authorized criteria—which is a pure question of constitutional law.

I will begin, as all constitutional analysis must begin, with the text of the Constitution governing impeachment. I will then examine why the Framers selected the words they did as the sole criteria authorizing impeachment.

In making my presentation, I will transport you back in time to a hot summer in Philadelphia and a cold winter in Washington. I will reintroduce you to patriots and ideas that have helped shape our great nation. To prepare for this journey, I have immersed myself in dusty old volumes from the 18th and 19th centuries. I ask your indulgence and attention as I quote from the wisdom of our founders. This return

to the days of yesteryear is necessary because the issue today is not what the criteria for impeachment *should* be—not what a contemporary legislative body *would* choose as the appropriate criteria—but what the Framers *actually chose* and what they expressly or implicitly rejected. I will ask whether the Framers would have accepted such vague and open-ended terms as "abuse of power" and "obstruction of Congress" as governing criteria. I will show, by a close review of the history, that they did not and would not accept such criteria, for fear that they would turn our new Republic into a British-style parliamentary democracy in which the chief executive's tenure would be—in the word of James Madison, the father of our Constitution —at the "pleasure" of the legislature.

The conclusion I will offer for your consideration is similar, though not identical, to that advocated by the highly respected Justice Benjamin Curtis—who dissented from the Supreme Court's notorious decision in Dred Scott, and who, after resigning in protest from the High Court, served of counsel to President Andrew Johnson in the Senate impeachment trial of 1868. He argued that "There can be no crime, there can be no misdemeanor without a law, written or unwritten, express or implied." In so arguing, he was echoing the conclusion reached by Dean Theodore W. Dwight of the Columbia Law School, who in 1867 wrote that the weight of legal authority supports the view that, "Unless the crime is specifically named in the Constitution —treason and bribery—impeach-

ments, like indictments, can only be instituted for crimes committed against the statutory law of the United States." The main thrust of my argument, however, is that even if this position is not accepted—even if criminal conduct were not required —the Framers of our Constitution implicitly rejected, and if it had been put to them directly, would have explicitly rejected, such vague terms as "abuse of power" and "obstruction of Congress" as among the "enumerated" and "defined" criteria for impeaching a president.

Justice Curtis's Argument in the Senate Trial of President Andrew Johnson

Among the articles of impeachment against President Johnson were accusations

of non-criminal but outrageous misbehavior, including ones akin to abuse of power and obstruction of Congress. For example, Article 10 charged that Johnson "did attempt to bring into disgrace, ridicule, hatred, contempt and reproach, the Congress of the United States . . ." Article 11 charged Johnson with denying that Congress was "[a]uthorized by the Constitution to exercise legislative power" and denying that "[t]he legislation of said Congress was obligatory upon him." Here is how Justice Curtis responded to these non-criminal articles:

> "My first position is, that when the Constitution speaks of 'treason, bribery, and other high crimes and misdemeanors' it refers to, and includes

only, high criminal offenses against the United States, made so by some law of the United States existing when the acts complained of were done, and I say that this is plainly to be inferred from each and every provision of the Constitution on the subject of impeachment."

Justice Curtis' interpretation is supported—indeed, in his view, compelled—by the constitutional text: Treason, bribery or other high crimes and misdemeanors. Treason and bribery are high crimes. 'Other' high crimes and misdemeanors must be akin to treason and bribery.

Curtis cited the Latin phrase "Noscitur a sociis," referring to a classic rule of interpretation that when the meaning of a word that is part of a

group is uncertain, you should look to the other words in that group that provide interpretative context. The late Justice Antonin Scalia gave the following example: "If one speaks of Mickey Mantle, Rocky Marciano, Michael Jordan and other great competitors, the last noun does not reasonably refer to Sam Walton (a great competitor in the market) or Napoleon (a great competitor on the battlefield)." Applying that rule to the group of words "treason, bribery or other high crimes and misdemeanors," the last five words should be interpreted to include only serious criminal behavior akin to treason and bribery.

Justice Curtis then reviewed other clauses in the Constitution related to impeachment that supported his view:

First, "The president of the United States shall have the power to grant reprieves and pardons *for offenses against the United States, except in cases of impeachment.*"

He cogently argued that if impeachments were not for "offenses against the United States," there would have been no need for a constitutional exception.

Second, "The trial of all *crimes, except in cases of impeachment,* shall be by jury." (Emphasis Added)

This demonstrated, according to Curtis, that impeachment requires a crime, but unlike other crimes, it does not require a jury trial. He also pointed out that an impeachment trial, by the "express words" of the Constitution, requires an "*acquittal* or a *conviction*"—judgments generally rendered only in trials for crimes.

Of course, President Johnson's lawyers argued in the alternative, as lawyers generally do in cases involving disputed facts and law: that Johnson did not violate the Articles of Impeachment; but even if he did, that the Articles did not charge impeachable offenses. Justice Curtis's "first position," however, was that the Articles did not charge an impeachable offense, because

they did not allege "high criminal offenses against the United States."

According to Professor Nikolas Bowie—who favors impeachment in this case[2]—Curtis's constitutional arguments were persuasive to at least some Senators "who were no friends of President Johnson," including the co-authors of the 13th and 14th Amendments. As Senator William Pitt Fessenden later put it: "Judge Curtis gave us the law, and we followed it." Senator James W. Grimes echoed Curtis's argument by refusing to "accept an interpretation" of high crimes and misdemeanors that change "according to the law of each Senator's judgment, enacted in

---

2 Professor Bowie wrongly believes that "abuse of power" is a crime. It is not in the statute books and there are no federal common-law crimes.

his own bosom, after the alleged commission of the offense." Though he wanted to see President Johnson, whom he despised, out of office, he believed that an impeachment and removal without the violation of a law would be "construed into approval of impeachments as part of future political machinery."[3]

According to Professor Bowie, Justice Curtis's constitutional arguments may well have contributed to the decisions by at least some of the seven Republican dissidents to defy their party and vote for acquittal —which was secured by a single vote.

I am not here arguing that current distinguished members of the Senate are bound by Justice Curtis's arguments, but I am suggesting,

3 *Harvard Law Review* Forum, Dec. 2018.

respectfully, that you should give them the serious consideration to which they are entitled by the eminence of their author and the role they may have played in the outcome of the closest precedent to the current case.

There may be a nuanced difference between the arguments presented by Justice Curtis and the position I have taken from my reading of the history. Curtis argued that there must be a specific violation of pre-existing law. He recognized that at the time the Constitution was adopted there were no federal criminal statutes on the books, because the national government had not yet been formed. This argument is offered by proponents of impeachment in support of the claim that the Framers could not have intended to limit the criteria for impeachment

to criminal-like behavior. Curtis addressed that argument head on: he pointed out that crimes such as bribery *would be* made criminal "by the laws of the United States, which the Framers of the Constitution knew must be passed." In other words, he anticipated that Congress would soon pass specific criminal laws punishing bribery and other serious crimes against the United States. The Constitution already included treason as a crime and defined it with specificity. He did not limit his definition of impeachable crimes to statutory offences. He included laws "written or unwritten, express or implied," by which he meant common-law crimes, which were recognized at the time the Constitution was adopted.

The position I have derived from the history

would include criminal-like conduct, akin to treason and bribery. There need not be allegations of a technical crime that would necessarily result in a criminal conviction. For example, if a President were to take a bribe outside of the United States, or beyond the period of the statute of limitations, he might not be subject to a criminal conviction in the United States. But he would be subject to impeachment for his criminal-like behavior. Or if a president committed extortion, perjury, or obstruction of justice, he could be charged with these crimes as impeachable offenses, because these crimes—though not specified in the Constitution—are *akin* to treason and bribery. This would be true even if some technical element (such as time and place) were absent. What Curtis and Dwight and I agree

on—and this is the key point in this impeachment case —is that purely non-criminal conduct, including abuse of power and obstruction of Congress, are *outside* the range of impeachable conduct.

This view is supported by text writers and judges close in time to the founding. William Oldnall Russell, whose 1819 *Treatise on Crimes and Misdemeanours* was a legal bible of the day, defined high crimes and misdemeanors as "such immoral and unlawful acts as are nearly allied, and equal in guilt, to a felony; and yet, owing to the absence of some *technical* circumstances, do not fall within the definition of a felony." Similar views were expressed by some state courts, though others disagreed.

Curtis's considered views—and those of

Dwight, Russell and others —based on careful study of the text and history, are not "bonkers," "absurdist," "legal claptrap," or other demeaning epithets thrown around by partisan supporters of this impeachment. Those who disagree with Curtis's textual analysis are obliged to respond with reasoned counter-interpretations, not name calling.

If Justice Curtis's arguments, and those of Dean Dwight, are rejected, proponents of impeachment must offer alternative principles and standards for impeachment and removal. In 1970, Congressman Gerald Ford, a man I admired, offered the following view in the context of impeaching a judge: "[A]n impeachable offense is whatever a majority of the House of Representatives considers it to be at a given

moment in history; conviction results from whatever offense or offenses two-thirds of the other body considers to be sufficiently serious to require removal of the accused from office . . ." He later said that this interpretation was inapplicable to the impeachment of a president.

Congresswoman Maxine Waters recently put it more succinctly, and in the context of a presidential impeachment: "Impeachment is whatever Congress says it is. There is no law." But this lawless view would place Congress above the law—above the Constitution itself. It is precisely the view expressly rejected by the Framers, who feared having a president serve at the "pleasure" of the Legislature, and it is precisely the view rejected by Senator James Grimes when he refused to accept an interpretation of high crimes and

misdemeanors that would change "according to the law of each senator's judgment enacted in his own bosom. . ." The Constitution requires, in the words of Gouverneur Morris, that the criteria for impeachment must be "enumerated and defined." Those who advocate impeachment today are obliged to demonstrate how the criteria accepted by the House in this case are enumerated and defined in the Constitution. The compelling textual analysis provided by Justice Curtis is confirmed by the debate in the Constitutional Convention, the Federalist Papers, and the writings of William Blackstone, which were heavily relied on by lawyers at the time of the Constitution's adoption.

Debates at the Constitutional Convention Regarding Impeachment

There were two great debates regarding impeachment of a president. The first was whether an elected president should be subject to impeachment at all. The second was if a president is to be subject to impeachment, what should the criteria be? These are very different issues, but they are often erroneously conflated.

During the broad debate about whether a president should be subject to impeachment, proponents of impeachment used vague and open-ended terms such as "unfit," "obnoxious," "corrupt," "misconduct," "misbehavior," "negligence," "malpractice," "perfidy," "treachery," "incapacity," "peculation," and "maladministration." They worried that a president "might pervert

his administration into a scheme of speculation or oppression," that he might be "corrupted by foreign influence" and—yes—that he might have "great opportunities of abusing his power." But no one suggested that these *general fears*, justifying the *need* for an impeachment-and-removal mechanism, should automatically be accepted as *specific criteria* for impeachment. Far from it, as Gouverneur Morris aptly put it: "[C]orruption and some few other offenses. . . ought to be impeachable, but . . . the cases ought to be *enumerated* and *defined*." The great fallacy of many contemporary scholars and pundits is that they fail to understand the critical difference between the *broad reasons* for *needing* an impeachment mechanism, and the carefully enumerated and defined *criteria* that should authorize the de-

ployment of this powerful weapon. A current hypothetical from Congress will illustrate this important difference. In a debate over regulating the content of social media, proponents of regulation might well cite many broad dangers, such as false information, inappropriate content, and hate speech. But when it came to enumerating and defining what should be prohibited, such broad dangers would have to be balanced against other important policies. The resulting legislation would be much narrower and more carefully defined than the broad dangers that necessitated some regulation. The Framers understood and acted on this difference.

And so, they got down to the difficult business of enumerating and defining precisely which offenses —among the many that they

feared a president might commit —should be impeachable, as distinguished from those left to the voters to evaluate.

Some Framers, such as Roger Sherman, wanted the President to be removable by "the National Legislature" at its "pleasure," much like a British Prime Minister can be removed by a simple vote of no confidence by Parliament. That view was rejected. Benjamin Franklin, "opposed decidedly the making of the executive the mere creature of the legislature." Gouverneur Morris was against "a dependence of the Executive on the Legislature, considering the Legislature"—you will pardon me for quoting this—"a great danger to be apprehended . . . ." James Madison expressed concern about the president

being improperly "dependent" on the Legislature. Others worried about "a feeble executive."

Hearing these and other arguments against turning the New Republic into a Parliamentary Democracy, in which the Legislature had the power to remove the president—a proposal made and rejected by Mr. Dickenson —the Framers set out to *strike the appropriate balance* between the *broad concerns* that led them to vote for a provision authorizing the impeachment of the president, and the need for *"specific" criteria* not subject to Legislative abuse or overuse. Among the criteria proposed were: "malpractice for neglect of duty," "mal conduct" or "neglect in the execution of his office," and "maladministration."

It was in response to that last term—a term used in Britain as criteria for impeachment — that Madison responded: "So vague a term will be equivalent to a tenure during pleasure of the Senate." Upon hearing Madison's objections, Colonel Mason withdrew "maladministration" and substituted "other high crimes and misdemeanors."[4]

Had a delegate proposed inclusion of "abuse of power" or "obstruction of Congress" as enumerated and defined criteria for impeachment, history strongly suggests that Madison would

---

4 He also added, "against the state." But soon thereafter, the words United States were substituted for the word State "in order to remove ambiguity." Ultimately the committee on style took out the words against the United States, apparently for stylistic rather than substantive reasons, and no vote was taken on that amendment.

have similarly objected and it would have been rejected.

Indeed, Madison worried that a partisan legislature could misuse the word "misdemeanor" to include a broad array of non-crimes, so he proposed moving the trial to the non-partisan Supreme Court. That proposal was rejected. This does not mean—as some have suggested—that Madison suddenly changed his mind and favored such misuse to expand the meaning of misdemeanor to include broad terms like misbehavior. Only that he feared it. His fear has been proved prescient by the misuse of the terms "high crimes" and "misdemeanors" by the House in this case.

The best evidence that the broad concerns cited by the Framers to justify impeachment

were not automatically adopted as criteria justifying impeachment is the manner by which "incapacity" was treated. Madison and others focused on incapacity as one of the primary reasons for authorizing a removal mechanism. But when it came to establishing criteria for removing a president, incapacity was not included, presumably because it is too vague and subjective a term. And when we had an incapacitated president near the end of Woodrow Wilson's second term, he was not impeached and removed. A Constitutional amendment—with carefully drawn procedural safeguards against abuse—was required to remedy the daunting problem of a president who is deemed incapacitated.

Another reason incapacity was not "enumerated and defined" as an impeachable offense is that it is not a crime to be incapacitated. It is not akin to "treason" or "bribery," and it is not a "high crime and misdemeanor." The Framers believed that impeachable offenses must be criminal in nature and akin to the most serious crimes. Incapacity simply did not fit in to this category, because there is nothing criminal about it. So the Constitution had to be amended to include a different category of non-criminal behavior that warranted removal.

Blackstone and Hamilton Support the Curtis View

There is no disagreement over the conclusion that the words "treason, bribery or other

high crimes . . ." require criminal behavior. The debate is over the words "and misdemeanors."[5]

The Framers of the Constitution were fully cognizant of the fact that the word misdemeanor was a species of crime. The book most often deemed authoritative was written by William Blackstone in Great Britain. Here is what he said in the version that was available to the Framers:

> A crime, or misdemeanor is an act committed or omitted, in violation of the law, either forbidding or commanding it. This general definition comprehends both crimes and misdemeanors; which,

---

5 The Framers wrote these words in conjunctive rather than disjunctive: high crimes and misdemeanors, not high crimes or misdemeanors. These words were intended to be read together, not separately.

properly speaking, are mere *synonymous* terms: though, in common usage, the word, "crimes," is made to denote such offenses as are of a deeper and more atrocious dye; while smaller faults, and omissions of less consequence, are comprised under the gentler name of "misdemeanors" only. (Emphasis added)

Blackstone also points out that not all misdemeanors were gentle. He cites several crimes—such as stealing certain pigs or fowl—that were "capital misdemeanors," punishable by death.

Moreover, Blackstone wrote that parliamentary impeachment "is a prosecution of already known and established law [presented] to the most high and Supreme Court of criminal juris-

diction. . ." He observed that "A commoner [can be impeached] but only for high misdemeanors: a peer may be impeached for any *crime*." This certainly suggests that Blackstone deemed high misdemeanors as a species of crime.

Hamilton is a little less clear on the criteria for impeachment because he was writing—in Federalist Number 65—more in defense of the Constitution as written, and less to define its provisions. But he certainly cannot be cited as in favor of criteria such as abuse of power or obstruction of Congress, nor of an impeachment voted along party lines. He warned of the "greatest danger": "That the decision will be regulated more by the comparative strength of parties, than by the real demonstrations of innocence or guilt." In addition to using the criminal terms

"innocence or guilt," Hamilton also referred to "prosecution" and "sentence." He cited the Constitutional provision that states that "the party convicted shall nevertheless be liable and subject" to a criminal trial, as a reason for not having the president tried before the Supreme Court. He feared a "double prosecution" before the same judiciary. These points all sound in criminal terms.

But advocates of a broad, non-criminal interpretation of "high crimes and misdemeanors," insist that Hamilton is on their side, citing the following words regarding the court of impeachment:

> "The *subjects of its jurisdiction* are those offenses which proceed from the mis-

conduct of public men, or, in other words, from the abuse or violation of some public trust. They are of a nature which may with peculiar propriety be denominated POLITICAL, as they relate chiefly to injuries done immediately to the society itself."[6] (Emphasis added)

---

6 They often neglect to quote the words that follow: "The prosecution of them for this reason, will seldom fail to agitate the passions of the whole community, and to divide it into parties more or less friendly or inimical to the accused. In many cases it will connect itself with the pre-existing factions, and will enlist all their animosities, partialities, influence, and interest on one side or the other, and in such cases there will always be the greatest danger that the decision will be regulated more by the comparative strength of parties, than by the real demonstrations of innocence or guilt.

These words are often misunderstood as suggesting that the *criteria* authorizing impeachment include "the misconduct of public men," or "the abuse or violation of some public trust." That is a misreading. These words were used to *characterize* the constitutional criteria that are "the subject of" the jurisdiction of the court of impeachment: namely "treason, bribery, or other high crimes and misdemeanors." Those specified crimes *are* political in nature, in that they are crimes that involve the "misconduct of public men" and "the abuse or violation of some public trust." Hamilton was not *expanding* the specified criteria to include—as independent grounds for impeachment —misconduct, abuse, or violation. If anything, he was *contracting*

them to require, *in addition* to proof of crimes, *also* proof that the crime must be of a political nature. This would exclude President Clinton's private, non-political crimes. In fact, Hamilton's view was cited by Clinton's advocates as *contracting*, not expanding, the meaning of "high crimes." Today, some of these same advocates, who now favor impeachment, are citing the same words as expanding its meaning.

Clinton was accused of a crime—perjury—and so the issue in his case was not whether the Constitution required a crime for impeachment. Instead the issue was whether Clinton's alleged crime could be classified as a "high crime" in light of its personal nature. During the Clinton impeachment, I stated in an interview that I did not think that a technical crime was required,

but that I did think that abusing trust could be considered. At that time, I had not done extensive research on that issue, because it was irrelevant to the Clinton case, and I was not fully aware of the compelling counter-argument. So I simply accepted the academic consensus on an issue that was not on the front burner at the time. Because *this* impeachment directly raises the issue of whether criminal behavior is required, I have gone back and read all the relevant historical material—as non-partisan academics should do —and have now concluded that the Framers did intend to limit the criteria for impeachment to criminal-type acts akin to treason and bribery, and certainly not extend it to vague and open-ended and non-criminal accusations such as "abuse of power" and "ob-

struction of Congress." I published this academic conclusion well before I was asked to present arguments to the Senate in this case.

Nor am I the only participant in the proceedings who has changed his mind. Congressman Nadler and Senator Schumer have expressed different views regarding the criteria for impeachment when the subject was president Clinton than they do now. When the President was Clinton, Professor Laurence Tribe, who is advising Speaker Pelosi, wrote that a sitting president could not be charged with a crime; he has now changed his mind.

If there are reasonable doubts about the intended meaning of "high crimes and misdemeanors," Senators might consider resolving such doubts by the rule of lenity. "Lenity" is a

traditional rule of interpretation that originated in Great Britain well before the Constitutional Convention and was well known to its legal members. It required that in construing a criminal statute that is capable of more than one reasonable interpretation, the interpretation that favors the defendant should be selected, unless it conflicts with the intent of the statute. It has been applied by Chief Justice John Marshall, Justice Oliver Wendell Holmes, Felix Frankfurter, Antonin Scalia, and others.

Applying this rule of interpretation to the words "high crimes and misdemeanors," would require that they be construed narrowly to require criminal-like conduct akin to "treason and bribery," rather than broadly to encompass "abuse of power" and "obstruction of Congress."

In other words, if Senators are in doubt about the meaning of high crimes and misdemeanors, the rule of lenity should incline them toward accepting a narrow rather than broad interpretation. Even if the rule of lenity is not strictly applicable to cases of impeachment—as distinguished from ordinary criminal cases—the policies underlying it reflect a common-sense approach to the interpretation of laws that have a punitive effect, which impeachment plainly does.

"Abuse of power" is not an impeachable offense

Even if the Senate were to conclude that a technical crime is not required for impeachment, the critical question remains: do abuse of power and obstruction of Congress consti-

tute impeachable offenses? The relevant history answers that question in the negative. Each of these charges suffers from the vice of being "so vague a term [that] will be the equivalent of tenure at the pleasure of the Senate."

"Abuse of power" is an accusation easily levelled by political opponents against controversial presidents. In our long history, many great presidents have been accused of abusing their powers.

A listing of such presidents includes the following:

- George Washington: Refusal to turn over documents related to the Jay Treaty.
- John Adams: Signing and enforcing the Alien and Sedition laws.

- Thomas Jefferson: Purchasing Louisiana without Congressional authorization.
- John Quincy Adams: Suspending a treaty.
- Martin Van Buren: Threatening to veto any laws abolishing slavery: "The most indecent abuse of power, of which any American president was ever guilty."
- John Tyler: "Arbitrary, despotic and corrupt use of the veto power.
- James K. Polk: Abraham Lincoln accused Polk of *abusing the power* of his office, contemptuously disregarding the Constitution, usurping the role of Congress, and assuming the role of dictator."
- Abraham Lincoln: Lincoln's suspension of Habeas Corpus. Cong. Globe, 38th Cong., 1st Sess., at802 (Feb. 24, 1864)

(referring to Administration's action as "abuse of power".)

- Ulysses S. Grant: President Grant's attempt to annex the Dominican Republic was called "an infraction of the Constitution of the United States and a usurpation of power not conferred upon the President."
- Grover Cleveland: Republican platform: "We denounce President Cleveland for its partisan abuse of its powers. . . ."
- William McKinley: President McKinley's use of his pardon power was called an abuse of power.
- Theodore Roosevelt: "Leonard Wood has been advanced by Theodore Roosevelt, by *abuse of power* unparalleled in the his-

tory of the United States Army . . . ."

- William Taft: Accusing Taft of "abusing his power."
- Woodrow Wilson: "Mason Flays Wilson for abuse of power"
- Franklin Roosevelt: "The attempt of the federal government to tax state municipal securities by a simple statute—as proposed by President Roosevelt—is a dangerous abuse of power . . . .
- Harry Truman: "Republican leaders in Congress tonight labeled President Truman's extra session calls a *'flagrant abuse'*of the Presidential emergency powers . . . ."
- Jimmy Carter: "President Carter's Rose Garden reelection strategy represents

a '*cynical abuse of presidential power*,' Republican presidential hopeful George Bush charged today."

- Ronald Reagan: Concerning Iran-Contra, Professor Laurence Tribe said: "Therein lies what appears to be the most serious breach of duty by the President—a breach that may well entail an impeachable *abuse of power* . . . ."
- George H. W. Bush: "The following was released today by the Clinton/Gore Campaign: . . . In the past week, Americans have begun to learn the extent to which George Bush and his administration have *abused their government power* for political purposes."
- Barack Obama: The House Committee

on the Judiciary held an entire hearing titled "Obama Administration's Abuse of Power." *Obama Administration's Abuse of Power: Hearing before the Committee on the Judiciary, House of Representatives,* 112th Cong., 2d Sess. (2012).

By the standards applied to earlier presidents, nearly any controversial act by a chief executive could be denominated as "abuse of power." For example, past presidents have been accused of using their foreign policy and even war powers to enhance their electoral prospects. Presidents often have mixed motives that include partisan and personal benefits, along with the national interest. Professor Josh Blackman provided the following example:

In 1864, during the height of the Civil War, President Lincoln encouraged Gen. William Sherman to allow soldiers in the field to return to Indiana to vote. What was Lincoln's primary motivation? He wanted to make sure that the government of Indiana remained in the hands of Republican loyalists who would continue the war until victory. Lincoln's request risked undercutting the military effort by depleting the ranks. Moreover, during this time, soldiers from the remaining states faced greater risks than did the returning Hoosiers.

Lincoln had dueling motives. Privately, he sought to secure a victory for his party. But the president, as a party leader and commander in chief, made a decision with life-or-death consequences.

Professor Blackman drew the following relevant conclusion from this and other historical events:

Politicians routinely promote their understanding of the general welfare, while, in the back of their minds, considering how these actions will affect their popularity. Often, the two concepts overlap: What's good for the country is good for the official's re-election. All politicians understand this dynamic.

80

Like all human beings, presidents and other politicians persuade themselves that actions seen by their opponents as self-serving are primarily in the national interest. In order to conclude that such mixed-motive actions constitute an abuse of power, opponents must psychoanalyze the president and attribute to him a singular self-serving motive.[7] Such a subjective probing of motives cannot be the legal basis for a serious accusation of abuse of power that could result

---

7 This is not like bribery statute, under which if a legislator took money in exchange for a vote, the fact that the vote may have been in the public interest is not a defense. Nor is this like a hypothetical situation in which a public official, even a president, conditions the release of funds to a foreign country on a promise to kickback some of those funds to the official. That would constitute several crimes.

in the removal of a duly elected president. Yet this is precisely what the managers are arguing: Whether the president's real reasons, the ones actually in his mind at the time, were legitimate.[8]

Even if a president were to demand a quid-pro-quo as a condition to sending aid to a foreign country—a highly disputed matter in this case—that would not, by itself, constitute an abuse of power. Consider the following hypothetical cases: A Democratic president tells Israel that foreign aid authorized by Congress will not be sent—or an Oval Office meeting will not be scheduled—unless they stop settlement building. I might disapprove of such a quid-pro-

---

8 House Justice Committee Report, page 33.

quo demand on *policy* grounds, but it would not be an abuse of power.

The claim that foreign policy decisions can be deemed abuses of power based on subjective opinions about mixed or sole motives—that the president was interested in *only* helping him-self —demonstrates the dangers of employing the vague, subjective, and politically malleable phrase "abuse of power" as a constitutionally permissible criteria for removal of a president. It follows that if a president—any president—actually did what John Bolton alleged this president did, that would not constitute an impeachable offense. Nothing in the alleged Bolton reve-lations—even if accurate—would change the constitutional calculus.

It is inconceivable that the Framers would have intended so politically loaded and promiscuously deployed a term as "abuse of power" to be weaponized as a tool of impeachment. It is precisely the kind of vague, open-ended, and subjective term that the Framers feared and rejected.

Consider the term maladministration. It is comparable in many ways to abuse of power. But there is a relevant difference. Blackstone denominated maladministration as a "high misdemeanor" that is "punished by the method of parliamentary impeachment," wherein such penalties, short of death, are inflicted." (p.121) These included "imprisonment."

Despite this British history, Madison insisted that it be rejected as a constitutional criterion

for impeachment because it is "so vague a term [that] will be equivalent to a tenure during pleasure of the Senate." And it was explicitly rejected and withdrawn by its sponsor.

This important episode in our constitutional history supports the conclusion that the Framers did not accept, whole hog, the British approach to impeachment, as some have mistakenly argued. Specifically, they rejected vague and open-ended criteria, even those that carried the punishment of imprisonment in Britain, because they did not want to turn our New Republic into a British-style parliamentary democracy in which the Chief Executive served "during pleasure" of the Legislature. The Framers would never have included—and did not include—abuse of power as an enumerated and defined criterion

for impeachment. By explicitly rejecting "maladministration," they implicitly rejected "abuse of power."

Nor would the Framers have included "obstruction of Congress" as among the "enumerated and defined" criteria. It, too, is vague and indefinable, especially in a constitutional system in which, according to Hamilton in Federalist 78, "the legislative body" is not themselves "the constitutional judge of their own powers," and the "construction they put upon them" is not "conclusive upon other departments." Instead, "the courts were designed to be an intermediate body between the people [as "declared in the constitution"] and the legislature," in order "to keep the latter within the limits assigned to their authority."

Under our system of separation of powers and checks and balances, it cannot be an "obstruction of Congress" for a president to demand judicial review of legislative subpoenas before they are complied with. The legislature is not the "constitutional judge of their own powers," including the power to issue subpoenas. The courts were designed to resolve disputes between the executive and legislative branches, and it cannot be an obstruction to invoke the constitutional power of the courts to do so.

By their very nature, abuse of power and obstruction of Congress are standardless. Both are subjective matters of degree and amenable to varying partisan interpretations. It is impossible to know in advance whether a given action will subsequently be deemed to fall on

one side of the line or the other. Indeed, the same action, with the same state of mind, can be deemed abusive or obstructive when done by *one person* but not by *another*. A few examples will illustrate the dangers of standardless impeachment criteria. Professor Noah Feldman has argued that a Tweet containing what he believed was false information could "get the current president impeached," if it is "part of a broader course of conduct." Professor Allan Lichtman has argued that the president could be impeached based on his climate change policy, which he regards as a "crime against humanity." I disagree with the president's climate policies (as well as many of his other policies), but such disagreements over policies, while proper bases

for a citizen deciding how to vote, are not a constitutional basis for impeachment.

Professor Tribe has argued that under the criteria of "abuse of power," President Ronald Reagan should have been impeached. Would any American accept a legal system in which prosecutors could charge a citizen with "abusive" conduct? Fortunately, we have constitutional protections against a statute that "either forbids or requires the doing of an act in terms so vague that men [and women] of common intelligence must necessarily guess at its meaning and differ as to its application." It's difficult to imagine terms that fit this description of what the Supreme Court has said "violates the first essential of due process," more closely than "abuse of power" and "obstruction of Congress."

Another constitutional rule of construction is that when words can be interpreted in an unconstitutionally vague manner or in a constitutionally precise manner, the latter must be chosen.

For the Senate to remove a duly elected president on vague, non-constitutional grounds, such as abuse of power or obstruction of Congress, would create a dangerous precedent and "be construed," in the words of Senator James N. Grimes, "into approval of impeachment as part of future political machinery." This is a realistic threat to all future presidents who serve with an opposing legislative majority that could easily concoct vague charges of abuse or obstruction. The fact that the long list of presidents who were accused of abuse of power were not impeached

demonstrates how selectively this term has and can be used in the context of impeachment.

Nor are these vague, open-ended, and unconstitutional articles of impeachment charged here saved by the inclusion in these articles of somewhat more specific, but still not criminal-type, conduct. The specifications are themselves vague, open-ended, and do not charge impeachable offenses. They include such accusations as compromising national security, abusing the power of the presidency, and violating his oath of office. In any event, it is the *actual articles* that charge "abuse of power" and "obstruction of Congress"—neither of which are in the Constitution —on which you must vote, not the more specific list of "means" included in the text of the articles. An analogy to a crim-

inal indictment may be helpful. If a defendant were charged with committing "dishonesty," that indictment would be dismissed, because dishonesty is a sin, but not a crime —even if the indictment included a long list of more specific acts of dishonesty.

Nor can impeachment be based on a bunching together of non-impeachable sins, none of which—standing alone—meet the constitutional criteria. Only if at least one constitutionally authorized offense is proved can the Senate consider other conduct in deciding whether removal is warranted.

In their three days of argument, the House Managers tossed around words even vaguer and more open-ended than abuse and obstruction to justify their case for removal. These include

trust, truth, honesty, and finally "right." These aspirational words of virtue demonstrate the failure of the Managers to distinguish alleged political sins from constitutionally impeachable offenses. We all want our presidents and other public officials to live up to the highest standards set by Washington and Lincoln—though both of *them* were accused of abuse of power by their political opponents. The Framers *could* have demanded that all presidents must meet Congressman Schiff's standards of being honest, trustworthy, virtuous, and right in order to complete their terms. The Framers knew how to use the language of "good behavior" if they chose to. They used it in describing the tenure of judges, but not of the president. But they didn't choose "good behavior" because they understood hu-

man fallibility. As Madison put it: "If men were angels, no government would be necessary." And then, speaking of presidents and other public officials, "if angels were to govern men, neither internal or external controls on government would be necessary." The Framers understood that if they set the criteria for impeachment too low, few presidents would serve their terms. Instead, their tenure would be at the "pleasure" of the legislature, as it was in Britain. So, they set it high, requiring not sinful behavior—not dishonesty, distrust or dishonor—but treason, bribery, or other high crimes and misdemeanors.

I end this presentation with a non-partisan plea for fair consideration of my arguments and those made by counsel and managers on both sides. I willingly acknowledge that the

academic consensus is that criminal conduct is not required for impeachment, and that abuse of power and obstruction of Congress are sufficient: I have read and respectfully considered the academic work of my many colleagues who disagree with my view and the few who accept it. I do my own research and thinking and have never bowed to the majority on intellectual and scholarly matters. What concerns me is that during this impeachment proceeding, there have been few attempts to respond to my arguments—and those of Justice Curtis, Dean Dwight, and Professor Bowie, all of whom agree that criminal-type conduct is required—on their merits and possible demerits. Instead, they have simply been rejected with negative epithets.

I respectfully urge the Senators to ignore

these epithets and to consider the arguments and counter-arguments on their merits.

I offer as a criterion for evaluating conflicting arguments what I have long called "the shoe on the other foot test." It is a colloquial variation of the philosophical argument offered by the great twentieth century thinker, and my former colleague, John Rawls. It is simple in its statement but difficult in its application. As a thought experiment, I respectfully urge each of you to imagine that the person being impeached were of the opposite party of our current President, but that in every other respect the facts were the same.

I have applied this test to the constitutional argument I am offering today. I would be making the same constitutional arguments in oppo-

sition to impeachment on these two grounds, regardless of whether I voted for or against the president and regardless of whether I agreed or disagreed with his or her policies. Can the same be said for all of my colleagues who now support impeachment?

I first proposed the "shoe" test twenty years ago in evaluating the Supreme Court's decision in *Bush v. Gore* asking the Justices to consider how they would have voted had it been candidate Bush, rather than Gore, who was several hundred votes behind and seeking a recount. I now respectfully ask the distinguished members of the Senate to consider that heuristic test in evaluating the arguments you have heard in this historic chamber. It is an important test because how you vote on this case will serve

as a precedent for how other Senators—of different parties, different backgrounds and different perspectives—vote in future cases. Allowing a duly elected president to be removed on the basis of the standardless, subjective, and ever-changing criteria —"abuse of power" and "obstruction of Congress" —risks being "construed," in the words of Senator James W. Grimes (a Republican Senator from Iowa, who voted against impeaching President Andrew Johnson) "into approval of impeachments as part of future political machinery."

I am here today because I love my country and our Constitution —the greatest and most enduring document of liberty in the history of mankind. Everyone in this room shares that love. I respectfully urge you to not to let your

feelings about one man—strong as they may be—establish a precedent that would undo the work of our founders, injure the constitutional future of our children, and cause irreparable damage to the delicate balance of our system of separation of powers and checks and balances. As Justice Curtis said during the trial of Andrew Johnson: "A greater principle" is at stake "than the fate of any particular president." The fate of future presidents—of different parties and policies—is also at stake, as is the fate of our constitutional system. The passions and fears of the moment must not blind us to our past or future.

Hamilton predicted that impeachment would "agitate the passions of the whole community and enlist all their animosities, partialities, influence and interest on one or the other."

The senate was established as a wise and mature check on the passions of the moment, with a "deep responsibility to future times."

I respectfully urge the distinguished members of this great body to think beyond the emotions of the day and to vote against impeaching on the unconstitutional articles now before you. To remove a duly elected president and to prevent the voters from deciding his electoral fate on the basis of these articles would neither do justice to this president nor to our enduring Constitution.

Thank you for your close attention. It has been a great honor to address you on this important matter.

U.S. SENATE QUESTION AND ANSWER TRANSCRIPT

Introduction

As soon as I concluded my speech to the Senate, many senators came up and thanked me. One said it was the "best law school class" he ever had. Another said it had "elevated" the discourse. Yet another thanked me for keeping him awake. Even a lawyer for the managers said it was a good speech, though he disagreed with my conclusions.

The president called me the next morning to express appreciation. The media reaction

was, as expected, generally divided along party lines, with some anti-Trump pundits grudgingly acknowledging that my analysis may have persuaded some senators.

The day after my speech, President Trump was scheduled to unveil the Israel-Palestine peace plan. I had consulted with its authors on the plan, so my wife and I were invited to the White House for its unveiling. Our seats were directly behind that of Secretary of State Mike Pompeo, who had been one of my students. The president gave him credit for his role in the plan, and there was applause, which we joined in. I patted my former student on the back to show support. Then the president mentioned a controversy that had plagued Pompeo: he was accused of berating a reporter for National Public

Radio, who, he claimed, had mislead him. There were also reports that he had banned another NPR reporter from his government airplane. The president jokingly encouraged this behavior, which—if true—I would never condone. Nonetheless, I patted Pompeo on the back again, as Carolyn and I joined others in politely smiling at the president's humor. A CNN cameraman captured the pat on the back and the smiles, and the clip went viral, as did the condemnation of me for seeming to encourage Pompeo's alleged bad conduct. That, of course, was not my intention. I was simply showing support for a former student, who was doing good things in the Mid-East and was caught up in a controversy. My message was, essentially, "This too shall pass, so continue to do good things." But media pundits

portrayed the pat as "atta boy," keep fighting with the media. This episode should have put me on notice that CNN and other anti-Trump media were searching for any excuse or opportunity to trash me and undercut my credibility, since it was becoming apparent that my analysis was having some influence on at least some senators.

Carolyn was more perceptive than I was, and urged me to "leave while I was ahead." I had committed to go back to the Senate for one day of the sixteen-hour question and answer period. Carolyn saw this as a potential trap, in which Democratic senators would try to bait me into a misstep. I saw it as a challenge, so I stuck to my agreement and went back to the Senate to answer questions. As we will see, Carolyn turned

out to be right, as the anti-Trump media and senators twisted, distorted, and straight-out lied about what I said in response to the first question put to me by Senator Ted Cruz, also a former student. Herein are the questions put to me by Senators and my responses. Judge for yourself whether, in answering the first question, I said or implied what some senators and media pundits attributed to me: namely, that a president can do *anything* he wants—including committing serious crimes—as long as he believes it will help him get re-elected, and that his re-election would be in the public interest.

The CHIEF JUSTICE. The question is addressed to counsel for the President:[9]

As a matter of law, does it matter if therewas a quid pro quo? Is it true that quid pro quos are often used in foreign policy?

Mr. Counsel DERSHOWITZ. Mr. Chief Justice, thank you very much for your question.

Yesterday, I had the privilege of attending the rolling-out of a peace plan by the President of the United States regarding the Israel-Palestine conflict,

---

9 To watch or listen to this question as it happened, please scan this code, or visit https://www.youtube.com/watch?v=mRlgvJmTFBE&feature=youtu.be]

and I offered you a hypothetical the other day: What if a Democratic President were to be elected and Congress were to authorize much money to either Israel or the Palestinians and the Democratic President were to say to Israel "No; I am going to withhold this money unless you stop all settlement growth" or to the Palestinians "I will withhold the money Congress authorized to you unless you stop paying terrorists, and the President said "Quid pro quo. If you don't do it, you don't get the money. If you do it, you get the money"? There is no one in this Chamber who would regard that as in any way unlawful. The only thing that would make a quid pro quo unlawful is

if the quo were in some way illegal.

Now, we talked about motive. There are three possible motives that a political figure can have: One, a motive in the public interest, and the Israel argument would be in the public interest; the second is in his own political interest; and the third, which hasn't been mentioned, would be in his own financial interest, his own pure financial interest, just putting money in the bank. I want to focus on the second one for just one moment.

Every public official whom I know believes that his election is in the public interest. Mostly, you are right. Your election is in the public interest. If a President does something which he be-

lieves will help him get elected—in the public interest—that cannot be the kind of quid pro quo that results in impeachment.

I quoted President Lincoln, when President Lincoln told General Sherman to let the troops go to Indiana so that they could vote for the Republican Party. Let's assume the President was running at that point and it was in his electoral interests to have these soldiers put at risk the lives of many, many other soldiers who would be left without their company. Would that be an unlawful quid pro quo? No, because the President, A, believed it was in the national interest, but B, he believed that his own election

was essential to victory in the Civil War. Every President believes that. That is why it is so dangerous to try to psychoanalyze the President, to try to get into the intricacies of the human mind.

Everybody has mixed motives, and for there to be a constitutional impeachment based on mixed motives would permit almost any President to be impeached.

How many Presidents have made foreign policy decisions after checking with their political advisers and their pollsters? If you are just acting in the national interest, why do you need pollsters? Why do you need political advisers? Just do what is best for the

country. But if you want to balance what
is in the public interest with what is in
your party's electoral interest and your
own electoral interest, it is impossible
to discern how much weight is given to
one or the other.

Now, we may argue that it is not in
the national interest for a particular
President to get reelected or for a particular Senator or Member of Congress—
and maybe we are right; it is not in the
national interest for everybody who is
running to be elected—but for it to be
impeachable, you would have to discern
that he or she made a decision solely on
the basis of, as the House managers put
it, corrupt motives, and it cannot be a

111

corrupt motive if you have a mixed motive that partially involves the national interest, partially involves electoral, and *does not involve personal pecuniary interest.*

The House managers do not allege that this decision, this quid pro quo, as they call it—and the question is based on the hypothesis there was a quid pro quo. I am not attacking the facts. *They never allege that it was based on pure financial reasons. It would be a much harder case.*

If a hypothetical President of the United States said to a hypothetical leader of a foreign country: Unless you build a hotel with my name on it and unless you give me *a million-dollar kick-*

back, I will withhold the funds. *That is an easy case. That is purely corrupt and in the purely private interest.*

But a complex middle case is: I want to be elected. I think I am a great President. I think I am the greatest President there ever was, and if I am not elected, the national interest will suffer greatly. That cannot be. (Emphasis added.)

The CHIEF JUSTICE. Thank you, counsel.

Mr. DERSHOWITZ. Thank you, Mr. Chief Justice.

[This is the answer that was willfully distorted by the Democratic leaders and managers. Deliberately omitting my explicit reference to quos that "were in some way illegal" or "corrupt," they mis-

characterized my answer as saying that a president could do *anything*—even grossly *illegal* acts—as long as he does it to get re-elected in the public interest. See my responses on pages 157-172.]

* * *

The CHIEF JUSTICE. The question from Senator MANCHIN reads as follows:

The Framers took the words "high crimes and misdemeanors" straight out of English law, where it had been applied to impeachments for 400 years before our Constitution was written. The Framers were well aware when they chose those words that Parliament had

impeached officials for "high crimes and misdemeanors" that were not indictable as crimes. The House has repeatedly impeached, and the Senate has convicted, officers for "high crimes and misdemeanors" that were not indictable crimes. Even Mr. Dershowitz said in 1998 that an impeachable offense "certainly doesn't have to be a crime." What has happened in the past 22 years to change the original intent of the Framers and the historic meaning of the term "high crimes and misdemeanors?"

It is counsel for the President's turn. Mr. Counsel DERSHOWITZ. Mr. Chief Justice, Senators, what happened since 1998 is that I studied more, did more research, read more documents, and like

any academic, altered my views. That is what happens. That is what professors ought to do, and I keep reading more, and I keep writing more, and I keep refining my views.

In 1998 the issue before this Senate was not whether a crime was required; it was whether the crime that Clinton was charged with was a high crime. When this impeachment began, the issue was whether a crime was required.

Actually, 2 years earlier, in a book and then an op-ed, I concluded—not on partisan grounds—on completely academic grounds, that you could not impeach for abuse of power and that technical crime was not required but

criminal-like behavior was required. I stand by that view.

The Framers rejected maladministration. That was a prime criteria for impeachment under British law. Remember, too, the British never impeached Prime Ministers. They only impeached middle-level and low-level people.

So the Framers didn't want to adopt the British approach. They rejected it by rejecting maladministration. And what is a metaphor or what is a synonym for maladministration? Abuse of power. And when they rejected maladministration, they rejected abuse of power.

Mr. Congressman SCHIFF asked a rhetorical question: Can a President

engage in abuse of power with impunity? In my tradition we answer questions with questions, and so I would throw the question back: Can a President engage in maladministration with impunity?

That is a question you might have asked James Madison had you been at the Constitutional Convention. And he would say: No. A President can't engage in that with impunity, but it is not an impeachable crime. Maladministration is not impeachable, and abuse of power is not impeachable.

The issue is not whether a crime is required. The issue is whether abuse of power is a permissible constitutional criteria, and the answer from the history is

clearly, unequivocally no. If that had ever been put to the Framers, they would have rejected it with the same certainty they rejected maladministration.

* * *

The CHIEF JUSTICE. Thank you. Senator SHELBY's question is directed to counsel for the President:

How does the noncriminal "abuse of power" standard advanced by the House Managers differ from "maladministration"—an impeachment standard rejected by the Framers? Where is the line between such an "abuse of power" and a policy disagreement?

Mr. Counsel DERSHOWITZ. Mr. Chief Justice, I will address this.

Senators, thank you very much for that question because that question I think hits the key to the issue that is before you today.

When the Founders rejected maladministration—and recall that it was introduced by Mason and rejected by Madison on the ground that it would turn our new Republic into a parliamentary democracy where a Prime Minister—in this case, a President—can be removed at the pleasure of the legislature.

Remember, too, that in Britain, impeachment was not used against the Prime Minister . . . it was used against lower level people.

So maladministration was introduced by Mason, and Madison said no, it was just too vague and too general.

What is maladministration? If you look it up in the dictionary and you look up synonyms, the synonyms include abuse, corruption, misrule, dishonesty, misuse of office, and misbehavior.

Even Professor Nikolas Bowie, a Harvard professor who was in favor of impeachment, so this is an admission against interest by him—he is in favor of impeachment—he says abuse of power is the same as misconduct in office, and he says that his research leads him to conclude that a crime is required.

By the way, the Congressman was

just completely wrong when he said I am the only scholar who supports this position. In the 19th century, which was closer in time to when the Framers wrote, Dean Dwight of Columbia Law School wrote that the weight of authority—by which he meant the weight of scholarly authority and the weight of judicial authority—this was in 1867—"the weight of authority is in favor of requiring a crime." Justice Curtis came to the same conclusion. Others have come to a similar conclusion.

You ask what happened between 1998 and the current time to change my mind. What happened between the 19th century and 20th century to change the minds

of so many scholars? Let me tell you what happened. What happened is that the current President was impeached.

If, in fact, President Obama or President Hillary Clinton would have been impeached, the weight of current scholarship would clearly be in favor of my position because many of these scholars do not pass the "shoe on the other foot" test. These scholars are influenced by their own bias, by their own politics, and their views should be taken with that in mind. They simply do not give objective assessments of the constitutional history.

Professor Tribe suddenly had a revelation himself. At the time Clinton

was impeached, he said: Oh, the law is clear. You cannot—you cannot—charge a President with a crime while he is a sitting President.

Now we have our current President. Professor Tribe got woke, and with no apparent new research, he came to the conclusion: Oh, but this President can be charged while sitting in office.

That is not the kind of scholarship that should influence your decision.

You can make your own decisions. Go back and read the debates, and you will see that I am right that the Framers rejected vague, open-ended criteria—abuse of power.

And what we had was the manager

making a fundamental mistake again.
She gave reasons why we have impeachment. Yes, we feared abuse of power.
Yes, we feared criteria like maladministration. That was part of the reason.
We feared incapacity. But none of those
made it into the criteria because the
Framers had to strike a balance. Here
are the reasons we need impeachment,
yes. Now, here are the reasons we fear
giving Congress too much power. So
we strike a balance. How did they strike
it? Treason, a serious crime; bribery,
a serious crime; or other high crimes
and misdemeanors—crimes and misdemeanors akin to treason and bribery.
That is what the Framers intended. They

didn't intend to give Congress a license
to decide whom to impeach and whom
not to impeach on partisan grounds.

I read you a list of 40 American
Presidents who have been accused of
abuse of power. Should every one of
them have been impeached? Should
every one of them have been removed
from office? It is too vague a term.

Reject my argument about crime.
Reject it if you choose to. Do not reject
my argument that abuse of power would
destroy—destroy—the impeachment
criteria of the Constitution and turn
it, in the words of one of the Senators
at the Johnson trial, to make every
Member of the Senate, every Member

of Congress, be able to define it from within their own bosom.

We heard from the other side that every Senator should decide whether you need proof beyond a reasonable doubt or proof by a preponderance. Now we hear that every Senator should decide on abuse of power.

The CHIEF JUSTICE. Thank you, counsel.

Mr. Counsel DERSHOWITZ. Thank you, Mr. Chief Justice.

* * *

The CHIEF JUSTICE. Thank you.
The question from Senator RUBIO

and the other Senators is for counsel for the President:

How would the Framers view removing a President without an overwhelming consensus of the American people and on the basis of Articles of Impeachment supported by one political party and opposed by the other?

Mr. Counsel DERSHOWITZ. Mr. Chief Justice, thank you.

Senators, Alexander Hamilton addressed that issue very directly. He said the greatest danger of impeachment is if it turns on the votes of one party being greater than the votes of another party in either House. So I think they would be appalled to see an impeachment go-

ing forward in violation of the Schumer rule and the rules of other Congressmen that were good enough for us during the Clinton impeachment but seemed to have changed dramatically in the current situation.

The criteria that have been set out are so lawless, they basically paraphrase Congresswoman MAXINE WATERS, who said: There is no law. Anything the House wants to do to impeach is impeachable. That is what is happening today. That places the House of Representatives above the law.

We have heard much about, no one is above the law. The House of Representatives is not above the law. They

may not use the MAXINE WATERS—
Gerald Ford made the same point, but it
was about the impeachment of a judge.
Judges are different; there are many of
them. There is only one President.

But to use that criteria, that it is
whatever the House says it is, whatever
the Senate says it is, turns those bodies
into lawless bodies, in violation of the
intent of the Framers.

Manager SCHIFF confused my
argument when he talked about intent
and motive.

You have said I am not a constitutional lawyer, but you admitted I am
a criminal lawyer. And I have taught
criminal law for 50 years at Harvard.

There is an enormous distinction between intent and motive. If somebody shoots somebody, the intent is that when you pull the trigger, you know a bullet will leave and will hit somebody and may kill them. That is the intent to kill them. Motive can be revenge. It could be money. It almost never is taken into consideration, except in extreme cases. There are cases where motive counts.

But let's consider a hypothetical growing out of a situation that we have discussed. Let's assume that President Obama had been told by his advisers that it really is important to send lethal weapons to the Ukraine, but then

he gets a call from his pollster and his political adviser, who says: We know it is in the national interest to send lethal weapons to the Ukraine, but we are telling you that the left wing of your party is really going to give you a hard time if you start selling lethal weapons and getting into a lethal war, potentially, with Russia. Would anybody here suggest that was impeachable? Or let's assume President Obama said: I promised to bomb Syria if they had chemical weapons, but I am now told by my pollsters that bombing Syria would hurt my electoral chances. Certainly not impeachable at all.

So let me apply that to the current

situation. As you know, I said previously there are three levels of possible motive.

One is, the motive is pure—only interest is in the way of what is good for the country. In the real world, that rarely happens.

The other one is, the motive is completely corrupt—I want money, kickback.

But then there is the third one that is so complicated and that is often misunderstood. When you have a mixed motive—a motive in which you think you are doing good for the country, but you are also doing good for yourself. You are doing good for me; you are doing good for thee. You are doing good, and you

altogether put it in a bundle in which you are satisfied that you are doing absolutely the right thing. Let me give you a perfect example of that from the case.

The argument has been made that the President of the United States only became interested in corruption when he learned that Joe Biden was running for President. Let's assume hypothetically that the President was in his second term, and he said to himself: You know, Joe Biden is running for President. I really should now get concerned about whether his son is corrupt because he is not only a candidate—he is not running against me; I am finished with my term—but he could be the President

of the United States. And if he is the President of the United States and he has a corrupt son, the fact that he has announced his candidacy is a very good reason for upping the interest in his son. If he wasn't running for President, he is a has-been. He is the former Vice President of the United States. OK, big deal. But if he is running for President, that is an enormous big deal.

So the difference—the House managers would make—is whether the President is in his first term or in his second term, whether he is running for reelection or not running for reelection. I think they would have to concede that, if he was not running for reelection, this

would not be a cross motive but would be a mixed motive but leaning on the side of national interest. If he is running for reelection, suddenly that turns it into an impeachable offense.

The CHIEF JUSTICE. Thank you. Thank you, counsel.

* * *

The CHIEF JUSTICE. Thank you. The question from Senators DAINES, LANKFORD, and HAWLEY is for counsel for the President:

Over the past 244 years, eight judges have been removed from office by the U.S. Senate but never a President. The

eight judges have been removed for bribery, perjury, tax evasion, waging war against the United States, and other unlawful actions. How do the current impeachment articles differ from previous convictions and removals by the Senate?

Mr. Counsel DERSHOWITZ. Mr. Chief Justice, there is an enormous difference between impeaching and removing a judge, even a justice, and impeaching and removing a President. No judge, not even a Chief Justice, is the judicial branch. You are the head of the judicial branch, but there is a judicial branch.

The President is the executive

branch. He is irreplaceable. There isn't always a Vice President. Remember, we had a period of time when there was no Vice President. We needed a constitutional amendment.

So there is no comparison between impeaching a judge and impeaching a President. Moreover, there is a textual difference. The Constitution provides that judges serve during good behavior. That is the Congressman SCHIFF standard, and it is a great standard. We wish everybody served only during good behavior. But the Constitution doesn't say that the President shall serve during good behavior. The big difference is the President runs every 4 years, and the

public gets to judge his good behavior. Judges don't run, and so there is only one judge of the good behavior; namely, the impeachment process.

So to make a comparison is to make the same mistake that when people compare the British system to the American system. We have heard a lot of argument that we adopted the British system by adopting five words: "other high crimes and misdemeanors." Yes, those words may have been borrowed from Great Britain, but the whole concept of impeachment was not. First of all, impeachment no longer exists in Great Britain; but when it did, it only operated for low-level and middle-level

people. All the impeachment trials that have been cited involve this guy in India, this guy in the commerce, this guy here, this guy there—utterly replaceable people.

In the British system, on the other hand, you can get rid of the head of state—the head of government, rather, by a simple vote of no confidence. That is what the Framers rejected. The Framers rejected that for a President. And so the notion that we borrowed the British system has it exactly backward. We rejected the British system.

We did not want a President to serve at the pleasure of the legislature. We wanted the President to serve at the

pleasure of the voters.

Judges don't serve at the pleasure of the voters, so there needs to be different criteria and broader criteria, and those criteria have been used in practice. For the most part, judges have been impeached for criminal and removed for criminal behavior.

But take an example that was given. If a judge is completely drunk and incapacitated and cannot do his job, it is easy to imagine how a judge might have to be removed for that.

But the President—there is an amendment to the Constitution, the 25th Amendment, specifically provided because there was a gap in the Constitu-

tion. And, please, Members of the Senate, it is important to understand, your role is not to fill gaps that the Framers deliberately left open.

Good arguments have been made: Why is it important to make sure people don't abuse their power, people don't commit maladministration? But the Framers left open, left those gaps. Your job is not to fill in the gaps. Your job is to apply the Constitution as the Framers wrote it, and that doesn't include abuse of power and obstruction of Congress.

Thank you.

The CHIEF JUSTICE. Thank you, counsel.

* * *

The CHIEF JUSTICE. Thank you.

The question from Senator BLUNT and other Senators is for the counsel for the President:

What does the supermajority threshold for conviction in the Senate, created by the Framers, say about the type of case that should be brought by the House and the standard of proof that should be considered in the Senate?

Mr. Counsel DERSHOWITZ. Mr. Chief Justice, Senators, there were several debates among the Framers, of course: Should you have impeachment at all? We talked about that—what the criteria for impeachment should be. But

then there was another debate: Who should have the ultimate responsibility for deciding whether the President should be removed?

James Madison suggested the Supreme Court of the United States as a completely nonpartisan institution.

Alexander Hamilton was concerned about that issue, as well, but he said the Supreme Court would be inappropriate because the judicial branch should not become involved directly as a branch—OK to preside over the trial—because ultimately an impeached President can be put on trial for crimes if he committed crimes.

And Hamilton said that if he were

to be put on trial, he would then be put on trial in front of the same institution— the judiciary—that had already impeached him, and they might have a predisposition.

So in the course of the debate, it was finally resolved that the Senate, which was a very different institution back at the founding—obviously, Senators were not directly elected; they were appointed by the legislature. They were supposed to serve as an institution that checked on the House of Representatives— more mature, more sober, elected for longer periods of time, with an eye to the future, not so concerned about pleasing the popular masses.

Remember, the Framers were very concerned about democracy. Nobody ever called the United States a democracy—"a Republic, if you can keep it," not a democracy—very great concern about that.

And then, when it came time to assign it to the Senate, there was discussion about what the criteria and what the—obviously—vote should be. The selection of a two-thirds supermajority was plainly designed—plainly designed— to avoid partisan impeachments, plainly designed to effectuate the very wise philosophy espoused by the Congressman and the Senator during the Clinton campaign; that is, during the Clinton impeachment.

Never ever have an impeachment or removal that is partisan. Always demand that it be a widespread consensus, a widespread national agreement, and bipartisan support. What better way of assuring bipartisan support than requiring a two-thirds vote because almost in every instance, in order to get a two-thirds vote, you need Members of both parties.

The Johnson case was a perfect example. In order to get that vote, you needed not only the party that was behind the impeachment, but you needed people from the other side as well, and when seven Republicans dissented based, I believe, largely on

the arguments of Justice Curtis and others—arguments I paraphrased here the other day—it lost by merely one vote. The Clinton impeachment, if you remember correctly, achieved a 50/50 split. Am I right about that? I think I am right about that. And it only lost—and it could have been 51-to-49. It wouldn't have been enough.

So I think it is plain that not only does the two-thirds requirement serve as a check on the House, but I think it sends a message to every Senator. It sends a message even to those Senators who would favor impeachment to reconsider because if you are voting for a partisan impeachment, you are violating the spirit of the two-thirds requirement.

There are many institutions where at the end of the day—for example, political conventions—they seek a unanimous vote just to show unity. I would urge some Senators who favor impeachment to look at the two-thirds and say: If there is not going to be a two-thirds, there shouldn't be an impeachment, and therefore, we are going to vote against impeachment even though we might think that the criteria for impeachment has been satisfied.

Do not vote for impeachment, do not vote for removal, unless you think the criteria articulated by the Senator and the Congressman and, I believe, by the Constitution and by Hamilton are

met, namely, bipartisan, almost universal concern by the United States of America. That criteria is not met, and the two-thirds requirement really illustrates the importance the Framers gave to that criteria.

The CHIEF JUSTICE. Thank you, counsel.

* * *

The CHIEF JUSTICE. The question for counsel to the President, directed to Professor Dershowitz, by Senators WICKER, MCSALLY, and MORAN, is this:

Professor Dershowitz: You stated

during your presentation that the House grounds for impeachment amount to the "most dangerous precedent." What specific danger does this impeachment pose to our republic? To its citizens?

Mr. Counsel DERSHOWITZ. Thank you, Mr. Chief Justice. Thank you, Senators.

I came of age during the period of McCarthyism. I then became a young professor during the divisive time of the Vietnam war. I, as you, lived through the division during the Iraq war and 9/11 and following 9/11.

I have never lived at a more divisive time in the United States of America than today. Families have broken up. Friends don't speak to each other. Di-

alogue has disappeared on university campuses. We live in extraordinarily dangerous times. I am not suggesting that the impeachment decision by the House has brought that on us. Perhaps it is merely a symptom of a terrific problem that we have facing us and likely to face us in the future.

I think it is the responsibility of this mature Senate, whose job it is to look forward, whose job it is to ensure our future, to make sure the divisions don't grow even greater.

Were the President of the United States to be removed today, it would pose existential dangers to our ability to live together as a people. The deci-

sion would not be accepted by many Americans. Nixon's decision was accepted— easily accepted. I think that decisions that would have been made in other cases would be accepted. This one would not be easily accepted because it is such a divided country, such a divided time.

If the precedent is established that a President can be removed on the basis of such vague and recurring and openended and targeted terms as "abuse of power"—40 Presidents have been accused of abuse of power. I bet you all of them have. We just don't know some of the charges against some of them, but we have documentation on so many. If

that criteria were to be used, this would just be the beginning of a recurring weaponization of impeachment whenever one House is controlled by one party and the Presidency is controlled by another party.

Now the House managers say there are dangers of not impeaching, but those dangers can be eliminated in 9 months. If you really feel there is a strong case, then campaign against the President. But the danger of impeachment will last my lifetime, your lifetime, and the lifetime of our children.

So I urge you respectfully, you are the guardians of our future. Follow the constraints of the Constitution. Do not

allow impeachment to become a normalized weapon, in the words of one of the Framers. Make sure that it is reserved only for the most extraordinary of cases, like that of Richard Nixon. This case does not meet those criteria.

The CHIEF JUSTICE. Thank you, counsel.

DERSHOWITZ: I NEVER SAID PRESIDENT COULD DO ANYTHING TO GET REELECTED

Op-ed, *The Hill*, January 30th, 2020

Media pundits and partisan politicians have been deliberately distorting the argument I made in the Senate impeachment trial of President Trump this week. Taking advantage of the fact that most of their own readers or viewers did not actually watch the Senate question and answer session, they have mischaracterized my argument as if I claimed

that a president who believes his reelection is in the national interest can do anything.

I said nothing like that, as anyone who heard what I said can attest. What I said was in response to the argument of the House managers, which was that any action by a politician motivated in part by a desire to be reelected was, by its nature, corrupt. Moving to my response, I listed three broad categories of relevant motive, which are pure national interest to help the military, pure corrupt motive to obtain a kickback, and mixed motive to help the national interest in a way that can also help a reelection effort.

I said the third motive was often the reality of politics, and helping your own reelection effort cannot by itself necessarily be deemed corrupt. I laid out, as an example, the decision of

President Lincoln to send Indiana troops home from the battlefield so they would vote for his party in a state election. He genuinely believed that a victory for his party in Indiana was essential to the war effort, but he also knew it would help him politically.

I laid out another hypothetical in which President Obama promised to bomb Syrian military targets if President Assad used chemical weapons. He broke his promise. What it if turns out that one reason he broke his promise was that his political advisers warned him that bombing Syria would lose him votes among the hard left? My point was that these are complex issues and the Framers did not intend impeachment for mixed motive decisions that contain an element of personal partisan benefit.

Anyone watching my answer would know that it was in response to the claim by the House managers that any electoral benefit constitutes an impeachable quid pro quo. I pointed out how open ended that argument is since most politicians truly believe their reelections help the national interest. I never said or implied that any candidate could do anything to reassure his or her reelection, only that seeking help is not necessarily corrupt, citing the examples of Lincoln and Obama. My critics now have an obligation to respond to what I said, not create straw men to attack.

I am certain that the senators and those other Americans who watched the question and answer session understood the point I was making. Just because a politician has mixed

motives for his or her actions, including a desire for reelection which he or she believes is in the national interest, does not prove that politician is corrupt. Even Democrat Adam Schiff, the lead House manager, understood it and responded that there are cases in which mixed motives can be criminal if one of the motives was corrupt.

I am sure those talking heads who mischaracterized my argument knew what they were doing. They heard my Lincoln and Obama examples but, instead of responding to those on the merits, which they were unable to do, they decided to create an easy but false straw man which they could mock. The straw man is that I argued that President Trump could do anything he wanted as long as he believed his election was in the national interest.

Pundits and tweeters have given preposterous examples from kidnapping an opposing candidate to bribing voters and rounding up Democrats to tampering with ballot boxes, all of which are criminal, as were many of the impeachable offenses of President Nixon. My point was that if a president does something legally within his authority, like withholding aid, sending soldiers home, or breaking a promise to bomb Syrian military facilities if they use chemical weapons, the fact that he was motivated in part by his desire for reelection does not in itself constitute impeachable conduct.

Under the theory of motivation, the theory to which I was responding to the House managers, Joe Biden, who I admire and like, would be guilty even if a small part of his motivation

for having a Ukrainian prosecutor fired was to protect his son or the Ukrainian company that appointed his son as a paid board member. I believe Biden is a patriot who cares deeply about the national interest, but he also cares deeply about his own family. Under the dangerous theory of the House managers, he would have to be psychoanalyzed to determine the role each motive may have played in an entirely lawful action. This broad theory takes us down a dangerous road.

Mixed motives are always matters of degree and, if they become a criteria for impeachment, they can be used selectively against certain candidates and not others. That is the danger to which I was alluding. But instead of reporting this danger, the media could not resist deliber-

ately distorting and mischaracterizing it. This deliberate distortion is a symptom of our times. It also explains why dialogue and debate about controversial and interesting ideas are becoming much more difficult in our divisive age.

EPILOGUE
THE DERSHOWITZ DOCTRINE:
THE DANGER OF
DEMONIZATION BY
DISTORTION

In arguments on the Senate floor, Democratic leaders have put on trial what they call the "The Dershowitz Doctrine": namely, that a president can do anything—even commit serious crimes—as long as he believes his election was in the public interest. Congressman Adam Schiff described it as a "lawless" variation

on the "Nixon" doctrine that whatever a president does is, by definition, lawful. Senator Schumer said that under my doctrine, Nixon did not commit any impeachable offense, despite evidence of his numerous crimes. (Thus ignoring my explicit statement that I supported Nixon's impeachment.) Media pundits went even further: Joe Lockhart, former Press Secretary to President Bill Clinton, accused me of making arguments that would justify the genocides of Hitler and Stalin.

What, then, did I say to warrant such demonization? In response to a question on whether it matters "if there was a quid pro quo," I said that would depend on "if the quo were in some way unlawful." If the politician's motive was "corrupt"—for example, if he were seeking a

kickback—that would be an impeachable crime. But if his entirely lawful act had "mixed motives," including his re-election, that would not turn a lawful act into a crime or impeachable offense.

I went on to say that all politicians have mixed motives for their political actions: they act in the public interest with an eye toward their electability. I emphasized that if a politician does something that would otherwise be legal, the fact that he was motivated in part by personal political advantage would not, by itself, turn his legal actions into illegal corruption. Put another way, a self-serving political motive—a desire to be re-elected—is not necessarily a "corrupt" motive. I also said that if the politician sought anything—a "quo"—that were "in some

way illegal," that would "make a quid pro quo unlawful."

Indeed, the main thrust of my hour-long opening presentation was that a President *could* be impeached if he committed crimes or criminal-like behavior akin to treason, bribery, or other high crimes and misdemeanors—*regardless* of whether his claimed motive was the public interest.

I made this self-evident point in response to arguments by the House managers that mixed motives could turn innocent conduct into a crime, if any part of the motive was corrupt, and that a motive to help one's own re-election could be corrupt.

I never once suggested that if a politician believed that his reelection was in the public

interest, his criminal or impeachable conduct could somehow be excused. Both the *Wall Street Journal* and *The New York Times* got it right. The *Wall Street Journal* said the following:

> "The media claim[s] that defense lawyer Alan Dershowitz said a President can to anything to further his re-election as long as he thinks it is in the national interest. This isn't what he said. The Harvard professor said explicitly that a President be impeached for criminal acts."

The *Times* reported on my position as follows: "Some Democratic senators and other critics accused him of suggesting that even Nixon

was not impeachable, despite his clear crimes. But that accusation is incompatible with Mr. Dershowitz's main argument: that an impeachable 'high crime and misdemeanor' requires an indictable offense."

These accurate descriptions bear no relationship to the distorted mischaracterizations by Democratic politicians, media pundits, and anti-Trump academics, who should know better.

Why, then, the deliberate distortions? Because my actual arguments resonated with some Senators. How do I know? Because some have said so publicly, while others have told me privately. Senator James Inhofe tweeted: "I agree with Alan Dershowitz—a liberal Democrat— who explained so well that more witnesses won't change the fact that President Trump did not

commit a crime or an impeachable offense." And Senator Ted Cruz wrote: "[Dershowitz's] learned insight played a critical role convincing senators that the President's conduct did not rise to the Constitutional threshold of 'other high crimes and misdemeanors.'" When I was arguing that all politicians have mixed motives and that it would be dangerous to deem corrupt a motive to be re-elected, I could see the reaction of senators in the room. Several came over to me at the end of the session to express agreement. None suggested that I was in any way justifying criminal conduct by a president.

Perhaps the most disturbing consequence of distorting the so-called "Dershowitz Doctrine" into a justification for any and all presidential actions is that it may create a dangerous prec-

edent. Because of the persistent mischaracterization of the "Dershowitz Doctrine," the Senate vote to acquit may be taken as a confirmation that a president who believes his re-election is in the public interest can do anything he wants—even commit serious crimes—to help himself get re-elected. That is not what I said or believe. Nor is it the precedent the Senators who vote for acquittal intend to establish. If such an unfortunate president were to be set, don't blame me, because I don't believe in the "Doctrine" as mendaciously distorted by Democratic leaders. It would be entirely the responsibility of those who invented and publicized this bizarre caricature of the nuanced argument I actually made before the Senate.

The Constitution
OF THE United States

We the people of the United States, in Order to form a more perfect Union, establish Justice, insure domestic Tranquility, provide for the common defense, promote the general Welfare, and secure the Blessings of Liberty to ourselves and our Posterity, do ordain and establish this Constitution for the United States of America.

Article I

Section. 1. All legislative Powers herein granted shall be vested in a Congress of the United States, which shall consist of a Senate and House of Representatives.

Section. 2. The House of Representatives shall be composed of Members chosen every second Year by the People of the several States, and the Electors in each State shall have the Qualifications requisite for Electors of the most numerous Branch of the State Legislature. No Person shall be a Representative who shall not have attained to the Age of twenty five Years, and been seven Years a citizen of the United States, and who shall not, when elected, be an Inhabitant of that State in which he shall be chosen.

[Representatives and direct Taxes shall be apportioned among the several States which may be included within this Union, according to their respective Numbers, which shall be determined by adding to the whole Number of free Persons, including those bound to Service for a Term of Years, and excluding Indians not taxed, three fifths of all other Persons.][1] The actual Enumeration shall be made within three Years after the first Meeting of the Congress of the United States, and within every subsequent Term of ten Years, in such Manner as they shall by Law direct. The number of Representatives shall not exceed one for every thirty Thousand, but each State shall have at Least one Representative; and until such enumeration shall be made, the State of New Hampshire shall be entitled to chuse three, Massachusetts eight, Rhode-Island and Providence Plantations one, Connecticut five, New-York six, New Jersey four, Pennsylvania eight, Delaware one, Maryland six, Virginia ten, North Carolina five, South Carolina five, and Georgia three.

When vacancies happen in the Representation from any State, the Executive Authority thereof shall issue Writs of Election to fill such Vacancies.

The House of Representatives shall chuse their Speaker and other Officers; and shall have the sole Power of Impeachment.

Section. 3. The Senate of the United States shall be composed of two Senators from each State, [chosen by the legislature thereof,][2] for six Years; and each Senator shall have one Vote. Immediately after they shall be assembled in Consequence of the first Election, they shall be divided as equally as may be into three Classes. The Seats of the Senators of the first Class shall be vacated at the Expiration of the second Year, of the second

---

1: *Changed by section 2 of the Fourteenth Amendment.*

2: *Changed by the Seventeenth Amendment.*

174

Class at the Expiration of the fourth Year, and of the third Class at the expiration of the sixth Year, so that one third may be chosen every second Year; [and if vacancies happen by Resignation, or otherwise, during the Recess of the Legislature of any State, the Executive thereof may make temporary Appointments until the next Meeting of the Legislature, which shall then fill such Vacancies.][3]

No person shall be a Senator who shall not have attained to the Age of thirty Years, and been nine Years a Citizen of the United States, and who shall not, when elected, be an Inhabitant of that State for which he shall be chosen.

The Vice President of the United States shall be President of the Senate, but shall have no Vote, unless they be equally divided.

The Senate shall chuse their other Officers, and also a President pro tempore, in the Absence of the Vice-President, or when he shall exercise the Office of President of the United States.

The Senate shall have the sole Power to try all Impeachments. When sitting for that Purpose, they shall be on Oath or Affirmation. When the President of the United States is tried, the Chief Justice shall preside: And no Person shall be convicted without the Concurrence of two thirds of the Members present.

Judgment in Cases of Impeachment shall not extend further than to removal from Office, and disqualification to hold and enjoy any Office of honor, Trust or Profit under the United States: but the Party convicted shall nevertheless be liable and subject to Indictment, Trial, Judgment and Punishment, according to Law.

3: Changed by the Seventeenth Amendment.

Section. 4. The Times, Places and Manner of holding Elections for Senators and Representatives, shall be prescribed in each State by the Legislature thereof; but the Congress may at any time by Law make or alter such Regulations, except as to the Places of chusing Senators.

The Congress shall assemble at least once in every Year, and such Meeting shall be [on the first Monday in December,][4] unless they shall by law appoint a different Day.

Section. 5. Each House shall be the Judge of the Elections, Returns and Qualifications of its own Members, and a Majority of each shall constitute a Quorum to do Business; but a smaller Number may adjourn from day to day, and may be authorized to compel the Attendance of absent Members, in such Manner, and under such Penalties as each House may provide.

Each house may determine the Rules of its Proceedings, punish its Members for disorderly Behavior, and, with the Concurrence of two-thirds, expel a Member.

Each house shall keep a Journal of its Proceedings, and from time to time publish the same, excepting such Parts as may in their Judgment require Secrecy; and the Yeas and Nays of the Members of either House on any question shall, at the Desire of one fifth of those Present, be entered on the Journal.

Neither House, during the Session of Congress, shall, without the Consent of the other, adjourn for more than three days, nor to any other Place than that in which the two Houses shall be sitting.

Section. 6. The Senators and Representatives shall receive a Compensation for their Services, to be ascertained by Law, and

---

4: Changed by section 2 of the Twentieth Amendment.

paid out of the Treasury of the United States. They shall in all Cases, except Treason, Felony and Breach of the Peace, be privileged from Arrest during their Attendance at the Session of their respective Houses, and in going to and returning from the same; and for any Speech or Debate in either House, they shall not be questioned in any other Place.

No Senator or Representative shall, during the Time for which he was elected, be appointed to any civil Office under the Authority of the United States, which shall have been created, or the Emoluments whereof shall have been encreased during such time; and no Person holding any Office under the United States, shall be a Member of either House during his Continuance in Office.

Section. 7. All Bills for raising Revenue shall originate in the House of Representatives; but the Senate may propose or concur with Amendments as on other Bills.

Every Bill which shall have passed the House of Representatives and the Senate, shall, before it become a Law, be presented to the President of the United States; If he approve he shall sign it, but if not he shall return it, with his Objections to that House in which it shall have originated, who shall enter the Objections at large on their Journal, and proceed to reconsider it. If after such Reconsideration two thirds of that house shall agree to pass the Bill, it shall be sent, together with the Objections, to the other House, by which it shall likewise be reconsidered, and if approved by two thirds of that House, it shall become a Law. But in all such Cases the Votes of both Houses shall be determined by yeas and Nays, and the Names of the Persons voting for and against the Bill shall be entered on the Journal of each House respectively. If any Bill shall not be returned by the President within ten Days (Sundays excepted) after it shall have been presented to him, the Same shall be a Law, in like Manner as if he had signed it, unless the Congress by their Adjournment prevent its Return, in which case it shall not be a Law.

Every Order, Resolution, or Vote to which the Concurrence of the Senate and House of Representatives may be necessary (except on a question of Adjournment) shall be presented to the President of the United States; and before the Same shall take Effect, shall be approved by him, or being disapproved by him, shall be repassed by two thirds of the Senate and House of Representatives, according to the Rules and Limitations prescribed in the Case of a Bill.

Section. 8. The Congress shall have Power To lay and collect Taxes, Duties, Imposts and Excises, to pay the Debts and provide for the common Defence and general Welfare of the United States; but all Duties, Imposts and Excises shall be uniform throughout the United States;

To borrow Money on the credit of the United States;

To regulate Commerce with foreign Nations, and among the several States, and with the Indian Tribes;

To establish an uniform Rule of Naturalization, and uniform Laws on the subject of Bankruptcies throughout the United States;

To coin Money, regulate the Value thereof, and of foreign Coin, and fix the Standard of Weights and Measures;

To provide for the Punishment of counterfeiting the Securities and current Coin of the United States;

To establish Post Offices and Post Roads;

To promote the Progress of Science and useful Arts, by securing for limited Times to Authors and Inventors the exclusive Right to their respective Writings and Discoveries;

To constitute Tribunals inferior to the supreme Court;

To define and punish Piracies and Felonies committed on the high Seas, and Offenses against the Law of Nations;

To declare War, grant Letters of Marque and Reprisal, and make Rules concerning Captures on Land and Water;

To raise and support Armies, but no Appropriation of Money to that Use shall be for a longer Term than two Years;

To provide and maintain a Navy;

To make Rules for the Government and Regulation of the land and naval Forces;

To provide for calling forth the Militia to execute the Laws of the Union, suppress Insurrections and repel Invasions;

To provide for organizing, arming, and disciplining, the Militia, and for governing such Part of them as may be employed in the Service of the United States, reserving to the States respectively, the Appointment of the Officers, and the Authority of training the Militia according to the discipline prescribed by Congress;

To exercise exclusive Legislation in all Cases whatsoever, over such District (not exceeding ten Miles square) as may, by Cession of particular States, and the Acceptance of Congress, become the Seat of the Government of the United States, and to exercise like Authority over all Places purchased by the Consent of the Legislature of the State in which the Same shall be, for the Erection of Forts, Magazines, Arsenals, dock-Yards, and other needful Buildings;—And

To make all Laws which shall be necessary and proper for carrying into Execution the foregoing Powers, and all other Powers vested by this Constitution in the Government of the United States, or in any Department or Officer thereof.

Section. 9. The Migration or Importation of such Persons as any of the States now existing shall think proper to admit, shall not be prohibited by the Congress prior to the Year one thousand eight hundred and eight, but a Tax or Duty may be imposed on such Importation, not exceeding ten dollars for each Person.

The Privilege of the Writ of Habeas Corpus shall not be suspended, unless when in Cases of Rebellion or Invasion the public Safety may require it.

No Bill of Attainder or ex post facto Law shall be passed.

No Capitation, or other direct, Tax shall be laid, unless in Proportion to the Census or Enumeration herein before directed to be taken.[5]

No Tax or Duty shall be laid on Articles exported from any State.

No Preference shall be given by any Regulation of Commerce or Revenue to the Ports of one State over those of another: nor shall Vessels bound to, or from, one State, be obliged to enter, clear, or pay Duties in another.

No Money shall be drawn from the Treasury, but in Consequence of Appropriations made by Law; and a regular State-

---

5: *See Sixteenth Amendment.*

ment and Account of the Receipts and Expenditures of all public Money shall be published from time to time.

No Title of Nobility shall be granted by the United States: And no Person holding any Office of Profit or Trust under them, shall, without the Consent of the Congress, accept of any present, Emolument, Office, or Title, of any kind whatever, from any King, Prince, or foreign State.

Section 10. No State shall enter into any Treaty, Alliance, or Confederation; grant Letters of Marque and Reprisal; coin Money; emit Bills of Credit; make any Thing but gold and silver Coin a Tender in Payment of Debts; pass any Bill of Attainder, ex post facto Law, or Law impairing the Obligation of Contracts, or grant any Title of Nobility.

No State shall, without the Consent of the Congress, lay any Imposts or Duties on Imports or Exports, except what may be absolutely necessary for executing it's inspection Laws: and the net Produce of all Duties and Imposts, laid by any State on Imports or Exports, shall be for the Use of the Treasury of the United States; and all such Laws shall be subject to the Revision and Controul of the Congress.

No State shall, without the Consent of Congress, lay any Duty of Tonnage, keep Troops, or Ships of War in time of Peace, enter into any Agreement or Compact with another State, or with a foreign Power, or engage in War, unless actually invaded, or in such imminent Danger as will not admit of delay.

ARTICLE II

Section. 1. The executive Power shall be vested in a President of the United States of America. He shall hold his Office during the Term of four Years, and, together with the Vice President, chosen for the same Term, be elected, as follows:

Each State shall appoint, in such Manner as the Legislature thereof may direct, a Number of Electors, equal to the whole Number of Senators and Representatives to which the State may be entitled in the Congress: but no Senator or Representative, or Person holding an Office of Trust or Profit under the United States, shall be appointed an Elector.

[The Electors shall meet in their respective States, and vote by Ballot for two Persons, of whom one at least shall not be an Inhabitant of the same State with themselves. And they shall make a List of all the Persons voted for, and of the Number of Votes for each; which List they shall sign and certify, and transmit sealed to the Seat of the Government of the United States, directed to the President of the Senate. The President of the Senate shall, in the Presence of the Senate and House of Representatives, open all the Certificates, and the Votes shall then be counted. The Person having the greatest Number of Votes shall be the President, if such Number be a Majority of the whole Number of Electors appointed; and if there be more than one who have such Majority, and have an equal Number of Votes, then the House of Representatives shall immediately chuse by Ballot one of them for President; and if no Person have a Majority, then from the five highest on the List the said House shall in like Manner chuse the President. But in chusing the President, the Votes shall be taken by States, the Representation from each State having one Vote; a quorum for this Purpose shall consist of a Member or Members from two thirds of the States, and a Majority of all the States shall be necessary to a Choice. In every Case, after the Choice of the President, the Person having the greatest Number of Votes of the Electors shall be the Vice President. But if there should remain two or more who have equal Votes, the Senate shall chuse from them by Ballot the Vice President.][6]

The Congress may determine the Time of chusing the Electors, and the Day on which they shall give their Votes; which Day shall be the same throughout the United States.

No Person except a natural born Citizen, or a Citizen of the United States, at the time of the Adoption of this Constitution, shall be eligible to the Office of President; neither shall any person be eligible to that Office who shall not have attained to the Age of thirty five Years, and been fourteen Years a Resident within the United States.

[In Case of the Removal of the President from Office, or of his Death, Resignation, or Inability to discharge the Powers and Duties of the said Office, the Same shall devolve on the Vice President, and the Congress may by Law provide for the Case of Removal, Death, Resignation or Inability, both of the President and Vice President, declaring what Officer shall then act as President, and such Officer shall act accordingly, until the Disability be removed, or a President shall be elected.][7]

The President shall, at stated Times, receive for his Services, a Compensation, which shall neither be increased nor diminished during the Period for which he shall have been elected, and he shall not receive within that Period any other Emolument from the United States, or any of them.

6: *Changed by the Twenty-Fifth Amendment.*

7: *Changed by the Twenty-Fifth Amendment.*

Before he enter on the Execution of his Office, he shall take the following Oath or Affirmation:—"I do solemnly swear (or affirm) that I will faithfully execute the Office of President of the United States, and will to the best of my Ability, preserve, protect and defend the Constitution of the United States."

Section. 2. The President shall be Commander in Chief of the Army and Navy of the United States, and of the Militia of the several States, when called into the actual Service of the United States; he may require the Opinion, in writing, of the principal Officer in each of the executive Departments, upon any Subject relating to the Duties of their respective Offices, and he shall have Power to grant Reprieves and Pardons for Offenses against the United States, except in Cases of impeachment.

He shall have Power, by and with the Advice and Consent of the Senate, to make Treaties, provided two thirds of the Senators present concur; and he shall nominate, and by and with the Advice and Consent of the Senate, shall appoint Ambassadors, other public Ministers and Consuls, Judges of the supreme Court, and all other Officers of the United States, whose Appointments are not herein otherwise provided for, and which shall be established by Law: but the Congress may by Law vest the Appointment of such inferior Officers, as they think proper, in the President alone, in the Courts of Law, or in the Heads of Departments.

The President shall have Power to fill up all Vacancies that may happen during the Recess of the Senate, by granting Commissions which shall expire at the End of their next session.

Section. 3. He shall from time to time give to the Congress Information of the State of the Union, and recommend to their

Consideration such Measures as he shall judge necessary and expedient; he may, on extraordinary Occasions, convene both Houses, or either of them, and in Case of Disagreement between them, with Respect to the Time of Adjournment, he may adjourn them to such Time as he shall think proper; he shall receive Ambassadors and other public Ministers; he shall take Care that the Laws be faithfully executed, and shall Commission all the Officers of the United States.

Section 4. The President, Vice President and all civil Officers of the United States, shall be removed from Office on Impeachment for, and Conviction of, Treason, Bribery, or other high Crimes and Misdemeanors.

ARTICLE III

Section 1. The judicial Power of the United States, shall be vested in one supreme Court, and in such inferior Courts as the Congress may from time to time ordain and establish. The Judges, both of the supreme and inferior Courts, shall hold their Offices during good Behaviour, and shall, at stated Times, receive for their Services, a Compensation, which shall not be diminished during their Continuance in Office.

Section. 2. The judicial Power shall extend to all Cases, in Law and Equity, arising under this Constitution, the Laws of the United States, and Treaties made, or which shall be made, under their Authority;—to all Cases affecting Ambassadors, other public Ministers and Consuls;—to all Cases of admiralty and maritime Jurisdiction;—to Controversies to which the United States shall be a Party;—to Controversies between two or more States;—[between a State and Citizens of another

State;—]⁸between Citizens of different States;—between Citizens of the same State claiming Lands under Grants of different States, and [between a State, or the Citizens thereof, and foreign States, Citizens or Subjects.]

In all cases affecting Ambassadors, other public Ministers and Consuls, and those in which a State shall be Party, the supreme Court shall have original Jurisdiction. In all the other Cases before mentioned, the supreme Court shall have appellate Jurisdiction, both as to Law and Fact, with such Exceptions, and under such Regulations as the Congress shall make.

The Trial of all Crimes, except in Cases of Impeachment, shall be by Jury; and such Trial shall be held in the State where the said Crimes shall have been committed; but when not committed within any State, the Trial shall be at such Place or Places as the Congress may by Law have directed.

Section. 3. Treason against the United States, shall consist only in levying War against them, or in adhering to their Enemies, giving them Aid and Comfort. No Person shall be convicted of Treason unless on the Testimony of two Witnesses to the same overt Act, or on Confession in open Court.

The Congress shall have power to declare the punishment of Treason, but no Attainder of Treason shall work Corruption of Blood, or Forfeiture except during the Life of the Person attainted.

ARTICLE IV

Section. 1. Full Faith and Credit shall be given in each State to the public Acts, Records, and judicial Proceedings of every

---

8: Changed by the Eleventh Amendment.

other State; And the Congress may by general Laws prescribe the Manner in which such Acts, Records and Proceedings shall be proved, and the Effect thereof.

Section. 2. The Citizens of each State shall be entitled to all Privileges and Immunities of Citizens in the several States.

A Person charged in any State with Treason, Felony, or other Crime, who shall flee from Justice, and be found in another State, shall on Demand of the executive Authority of the State from which he fled, be delivered up, to be removed to the State having Jurisdiction of the Crime.

[No person held to Service or Labour in one State, under the Laws thereof, escaping into another, shall, in Consequence of any Law or Regulation therein, be discharged from such Service or Labour, But shall be delivered up on Claim of the Party to whom such Service or Labor may be due.][9]

Section. 3. New States may be admitted by the Congress into this Union; but no new States shall be formed or erected within the Jurisdiction of any other State; nor any State be formed by the Junction of two or more States, or Parts of States, without the Consent of the Legislatures of the States concerned as well as of the Congress.

The Congress shall have Power to dispose of and make all needful Rules and Regulations respecting the Territory or other Property belonging to the United States; and nothing in this Constitution shall be so construed as to Prejudice any Claims of the United States, or of any particular State.

Section. 4. The United States shall guarantee to every State in

---

9: *Changed by the Thirteenth Amendment.*

this Union a Republican Form of Government, and shall protect each of them against Invasion; and on Application of the Legislature, or of the Executive (when the Legislature cannot be convened) against domestic Violence.

ARTICLE V

The Congress, whenever two thirds of both Houses shall deem it necessary, shall propose Amendments to this Constitution, or, on the Application of the Legislatures of two thirds of the several States, shall call a Convention for proposing Amendments, which, in either Case, shall be valid to all Intents and Purposes, as Part of this Constitution, when ratified by the Legislatures of three fourths of the several States, or by Conventions in three fourths thereof, as the one or the other Mode of Ratification may be proposed by the Congress; Provided that no Amendment which may be made prior to the Year one thousand eight hundred and eight shall in any Manner affect the first and fourth Clauses in the ninth Section of the first Article; and that no State, without its Consent, shall be deprived of it's equal Suffrage in the Senate.

ARTICLE VI

All Debts contracted and Engagements entered into, before the Adoption of this Constitution, shall be as valid against the United States under this Constitution, as under the Confederation.

This Constitution, and the Laws of the United States which shall be made in Pursuance thereof; and all Treaties made, or which shall be made, under the Authority of the United States, shall be the supreme Law of the Land; and the Judges in every State shall be bound thereby, any Thing in the Constitution or Laws of any State to the Contrary notwithstanding.

The Senators and Representatives before mentioned, and the Members of the several State Legislatures, and all executive and judicial Officers, both of the United States and of the several States, shall be bound by Oath or Affirmation, to support this Constitution; but no religious Test shall ever be required as a Qualification to any Office or public Trust under the United States.

ARTICLE VII

The Ratification of the Conventions of nine States, shall be sufficient for the Establishment of this Constitution between the States so ratifying the Same.

Done in Convention by the Unanimous Consent of the States present the Seventeenth Day of September in the Year of our Lord one thousand seven hundred and Eighty seven and of the Independence of the United States of America the Twelfth.

In Witness whereof We have hereunto subscribed our Names,

Go. WASHINGTON

     Presid. and deputy from Virginia

     New Hampshire

John Langdon

Nicholas Gilman

     Massachusetts

Nathaniel Gorham

Rufus King

Connecticut

Wm. Saml. Johnson

Roger Sherman

New York

Alexander Hamilton

New Jersey

Will Livingston

David Brearley

Wm. Paterson

Jona: Dayton

Pennsylvania

B Franklin

Thomas Mifflin

Robt Morris

Geo: Clymer

Thos FitzSimons

Jared Ingersoll

James Wilson

Gouv Morris

Delaware

George Read

Gunning Bedford jun

John Dickinson

Richard Bassett

Jaco: Broom

Maryland

James Mchenry

Dan of St Thos. Jenifer

Danl Carroll

Virginia

John Blair

James Madison Jr.

North Carolina

Wm. Blount

Rich'd Dobbs Spaight

Hu Williamson

South Carolina

J. Rutledge

Charles Cotesworth Pinckney

Charles Pinckney

Pierce Butler

Georgia

William Few

Abr Baldwin

Attest:

William Jackson, Secretary

Amendments to the Constitution of the United States

AMENDMENT I.[1]

Congress shall make no law respecting an establishment of religion, or prohibiting the free exercise thereof; or abridging the freedom of speech, or of the press, or the right of the people peaceably to assemble, and to petition the Government for a redress of grievances.

AMENDMENT II.

A well-regulated militia, being necessary to the security of a free State, the right of the people to keep and bear Arms, shall not be infringed.

AMENDMENT III.

No Soldier shall, in time of peace be quartered in any house, without the consent of the Owner, nor in time of war, but in a manner to be prescribed by law.

AMENDMENT IV.

The right of the people to be secure in their persons, houses, papers, and effects, against unreasonable searches and seizures, shall not be violated, and no Warrants shall issue, but upon probable cause, supported by Oath or affirmation, and particularly describing the place to be searched, and the persons or things to be seized.

1: *The first ten Amendments (Bill of Rights) were ratified effective December 15, 1791.*

AMENDMENT V.

No person shall be held to answer for a capital, or otherwise infamous crime, unless on a presentment or indictment of a Grand Jury, except in cases arising in the land or naval forces, or in the Militia, when in actual service in time of War or public danger; nor shall any person be subject for the same offense to be twice put in jeopardy of life or limb; nor shall be compelled in any criminal case to be a witness against himself, nor be deprived of life, liberty, or property, without due process of law; nor shall private property be taken for public use without just compensation.

AMENDMENT VI.

In all criminal prosecutions, the accused shall enjoy the right to a speedy and public trial, by an impartial jury of the State and district wherein the crime shall have been committed, which district shall have been previously ascertained by law, and to be informed of the nature and cause of the accusation; to be confronted with the witnesses against him; to have compulsory process for obtaining witnesses in his favor, and to have the assistance of counsel for his defense.

AMENDMENT VII.

In Suits at common law, where the value in controversy shall exceed twenty dollars, the right of trial by jury shall be preserved, and no fact tried by a jury shall be otherwise re-examined in any Court of the United States, than according to the rules of the common law.

AMENDMENT VIII.

Excessive bail shall not be required nor excessive fines imposed, nor cruel and unusual punishments inflicted.

AMENDMENT IX.

The enumeration in the Constitution, of certain rights, shall not be construed to deny or disparage others retained by the people.

AMENDMENT X.

The powers not delegated to the United States by the Constitution, nor prohibited by it to the States, are reserved to the States respectively, or to the people.

AMENDMENT XI.[2]

The Judicial power of the United States shall not be construed to extend to any suit in law or equity, commenced or prosecuted against one of the United States by Citizens of another State, or by Citizens or Subjects of any Foreign State.

AMENDMENT XII.[3]

The Electors shall meet in their respective states and vote by ballot for President and Vice President, one of whom, at least, shall not be an inhabitant of the same state with themselves; they shall name in their ballots the person voted for as President, and in distinct ballots the person voted for as Vice President, and they shall make distinct lists of all persons voted for as President, and of all persons voted for as Vice President, and of the number of votes for each, which lists they shall sign and certify, and transmit sealed to the seat of the government of the United States,

---

2: *Passed by Congress March 4, 1794. Ratified February 7, 1795.*
Note: Article III, section 2, of the Constitution was modified by the Eleventh Amendment.

3: *Passed by Congress December 9, 1803. Ratified June 15, 1804.*
Note: A portion of Article II, section 1 of the Constitution was superseded by the Twelfth Amendment.

directed to the President of the Senate;—the President of the Senate shall, in the presence of the Senate and House of Representatives, open all the certificates and the votes shall then be counted;—The person having the greatest number of votes for President, shall be the President, if such number be a majority of the whole number of Electors appointed; and if no person have such majority, then from the persons having the highest numbers not exceeding three on the list of those voted for as President, the House of Representatives shall choose immediately, by ballot, the President. But in choosing the President, the votes shall be taken by states, the representation from each state having one vote; a quorum for this purpose shall consist of a member or members from two-thirds of the states, and a majority of all the states shall be necessary to a choice. [And if the House of Representatives shall not choose a President whenever the right of choice shall devolve upon them, before the fourth day of March next following, then the Vice President shall act as President, as in case of the death or other constitutional disability of the President—][4] The person having the greatest number of votes as Vice President, shall be the Vice President, if such number be a majority of the whole number of Electors appointed, and if no person have a majority, then from the two highest numbers on the list, the Senate shall choose the Vice President; a quorum for the purpose shall consist of two-thirds of the whole number of Senators, and a majority of the whole number shall be necessary to a choice. But no person constitutionally ineligible to the office of President shall be eligible to that of Vice President of the United States.

4: Superseded by section 3 of the 20th amendment.

AMENDMENT XIII.[5]

Section 1. Neither slavery nor involuntary servitude, except as a punishment for crime whereof the party shall have been duly convicted, shall exist within the United States, or any place subject to their jurisdiction.

Section 2. Congress shall have power to enforce this article by appropriate legislation.

AMENDMENT XIV.[6]

Section 1. All persons born or naturalized in the United States, and subject to the jurisdiction thereof, are citizens of the United States and of the State wherein they reside. No State shall make or enforce any law which shall abridge the privileges or immunities of citizens of the United States; nor shall any State deprive any person of life, liberty, or property, without due process of law; nor deny to any person within its jurisdiction the equal protection of the laws.

Section 2. Representatives shall be apportioned among the several States according to their respective numbers, counting the whole number of persons in each State, excluding Indians not taxed. But when the right to vote at any election for the choice of electors for President and Vice President of the United States, Representatives in Congress, the Executive and Judicial officers of a State, or the members of the Legislature thereof, is denied

---

5: *Passed by Congress January 31, 1865. Ratified December 6, 1865.*
Note: A portion of Article IV, section 2, of the Constitution was superseded by the Thirteenth Amendment.

6: *Passed by Congress June 13, 1866. Ratified July 9, 1868.*
Note: Article I, section 2, of the Constitution was modified by section 2 of the Fourteenth Amendment.

197

to any of the male inhabitants of such State, being twenty-one years of age,[7] and citizens of the United States, or in any way abridged, except for participation in rebellion, or other crime, the basis of representation therein shall be reduced in the proportion which the number of such male citizens shall bear to the whole number of male citizens twenty-one years of age in such State.

Section 3. No person shall be a Senator or Representative in Congress, or elector of President and Vice President, or hold any office, civil or military, under the United States, or under any State, who, having previously taken an oath, as a member of Congress, or as an officer of the United States, or as a member of any State legislature, or as an executive or judicial officer of any State, to support the Constitution of the United States, shall have engaged in insurrection or rebellion against the same, or given aid or comfort to the enemies thereof. But Congress may by a vote of two-thirds of each House, remove such disability.

Section 4. The validity of the public debt of the United States, authorized by law, including debts incurred for payment of pensions and bounties for services in suppressing insurrection or rebellion, shall not be questioned. But neither the United States nor any State shall assume or pay any debt or obligation incurred in aid of insurrection or rebellion against the United States, or any claim for the loss or emancipation of any slave; but all such debts, obligations and claims shall be held illegal and void.

Section 5. The Congress shall have the power to enforce, by appropriate legislation, the provisions of this article.

7: *Changed by section 1 of the Twenty-Sixth amendment.*

AMENDMENT XV.[8]

Section 1. The right of citizens of the United States to vote shall not be denied or abridged by the United States or by any State on account of race, color, or previous condition of servitude.

Section 2. The Congress shall have the power to enforce this article by appropriate legislation.

AMENDMENT XVI[9]

The Congress shall have power to lay and collect taxes on incomes, from whatever source derived, without apportionment among the several States, and without regard to any census or enumeration.

AMENDMENT XVII.[10]

The Senate of the United States shall be composed of two Senators from each State, elected by the people thereof, for six years; and each Senator shall have one vote. The electors in each State shall have the qualifications requisite for electors of the most numerous branch of the State legislatures.

When vacancies happen in the representation of any State in the Senate, the executive authority of such State shall issue writs of election to fill such vacancies: Provided, That the legislature of any State may empower the executive thereof to make

---

8: *Passed by Congress February 26, 1869. Ratified February 3, 1870.*

9: *Passed by Congress July 2, 1909. Ratified February 3, 1913.*
Note: Article I, section 9, of the Constitution was modified by Sixteenth Amendment.

10: *Passed by Congress May 13, 1912. Ratified April 8, 1913.*
Note: Article I, section 3, of the Constitution was modified by the Seventeenth Amendment.

temporary appointments until the people fill the vacancies by election as the legislature may direct.

This amendment shall not be so construed as to affect the election or term of any Senator chosen before it becomes valid as part of the Constitution.

AMENDMENT XVIII.[11]

Section 1. After one year from the ratification of this article the manufacture, sale, or transportation of intoxicating liquors within, the importation thereof into, or the exportation thereof from the United States and all territory subject to the jurisdiction thereof for beverage purposes is hereby prohibited.

Section 2. The Congress and the several States shall have concurrent power to enforce this article by appropriate legislation.

Section 3. This article shall be inoperative unless it shall have been ratified as an amendment to the Constitution by the legislatures of the several States, as provided in the Constitution, within seven years from the date of the submission hereof to the States by the Congress.

AMENDMENT XIX.[12]

The right of citizens of the United States to vote shall not be denied or abridged by the United States or by any State on account of sex.

Congress shall have power to enforce this article by appropriate legislation.

11: *Passed by Congress December 18, 1917. Ratified January 16, 1919. Repealed by the Twenty-First Amendment.*

12: *Passed by Congress June 4, 1919. Ratified August 18, 1920.*

AMENDMENT XX.[13]

Section 1. The terms of the President and the Vice President shall end at noon on the 20th day of January, and the terms of Senators and Representatives at noon on the 3d day of January, of the years in which such terms would have ended if this article had not been ratified; and the terms of their successors shall then begin.

Section 2. The Congress shall assemble at least once in every year, and such meeting shall begin at noon on the 3d day of January, unless they shall by law appoint a different day.

Section 3. If, at the time fixed for the beginning of the term of the President, the President elect shall have died, the Vice President elect shall become President. If a President shall not have been chosen before the time fixed for the beginning of his term, or if the President elect shall have failed to qualify, then the Vice President elect shall act as President until a President shall have qualified; and the Congress may by law provide for the case wherein neither a President elect nor a Vice President elect shall have qualified, declaring who shall then act as President, or the manner in which one who is to act shall be selected, and such person shall act accordingly until a President or Vice President shall have qualified.

Section 4. The Congress may by law provide for the case of the death of any of the persons from whom the House of Representatives may choose a President whenever the right of choice shall have devolved upon them, and for the case of the death of

---

13: *Passed by Congress March 2, 1932. Ratified January 23, 1933.*
Note: Article I, section 4, of the Constitution was modified by section 2 of this amendment. In addition, a portion of the Twelfth Amendment was superseded by section 3.

any of the persons from whom the Senate may choose a Vice President whenever the right of choice shall have devolved upon them.

Section 5. Sections 1 and 2 shall take effect on the 15th day of October following the ratification of this article.

Section 6. This article shall be inoperative unless it shall have been ratified as an amendment to the Constitution by the legislatures of three-fourths of the several States within seven years from the date of its submission.

AMENDMENT XXI.[14]

Section 1. The eighteenth article of amendment to the Constitution of the United States is hereby repealed.

Section 2. The transportation or importation into any State, Territory, or possession of the United States for delivery or use therein of intoxicating liquors, in violation of the laws thereof, is hereby prohibited.

Section 3. This article shall be inoperative unless it shall have been ratified as an amendment to the Constitution by conventions in the several States, as provided in the Constitution, within seven years from the date of the submission hereof to the States by the Congress.

AMENDMENT XXII.[15]

Section 1. No person shall be elected to the office of the President more than twice, and no person who has held the office of President, or acted as President, for more than two years of

---

14: *Passed by Congress February 20, 1933. Ratified December 5, 1933.*

15: *Passed by Congress March 21, 1947. Ratified February 27, 1951.*

a term to which some other person was elected President shall be elected to the office of the President more than once. But this Article shall not apply to any person holding the office of President when this Article was proposed by the Congress, and shall not prevent any person who may be holding the office of President, or acting as President, during the term within which this Article becomes operative from holding the office of President or acting as President during the remainder of such term.

Section 2. This article shall be inoperative unless it shall have been ratified as an amendment to the Constitution by the legislatures of three-fourths of the several States within seven years from the date of its submission to the States by the Congress.

AMENDMENT XXIII.[16]

Section 1. The District constituting the seat of Government of the United States shall appoint in such manner as the Congress may direct:

A number of electors of President and Vice President equal to the whole number of Senators and Representatives in Congress to which the District would be entitled if it were a State, but in no event more than the least populous State; they shall be in addition to those appointed by the States, but they shall be considered, for the purposes of the election of President and Vice President, to be electors appointed by a State; and they shall meet in the District and perform such duties as provided by the twelfth article of amendment.

Section 2. The Congress shall have power to enforce this article by appropriate legislation.

16: *Passed by Congress June 16, 1960. Ratified March 29, 1961.*

AMENDMENT XXIV.[17]

Section 1. The right of citizens of the United States to vote in any primary or other election for President or Vice President, for electors for President or Vice President, or for Senator or Representative in Congress, shall not be denied or abridged by the United States or any State by reason of failure to pay any poll tax or other tax.

Section 2. The Congress shall have power to enforce this article by appropriate legislation.

AMENDMENT XXV.[18]

Section 1. In case of the removal of the President from office or of his death or resignation, the Vice President shall become President.

Section 2. Whenever there is a vacancy in the office of the Vice President, the President shall nominate a Vice President who shall take office upon confirmation by a majority vote of both Houses of Congress.

Section 3. Whenever the President transmits to the President pro tempore of the Senate and the Speaker of the House of Representatives his written declaration that he is unable to discharge the powers and duties of his office, and until he transmits to them a written declaration to the contrary, such powers and duties shall be discharged by the Vice President as Acting President.

17: *Passed by Congress August 27, 1962. Ratified January 23, 1964.*

18: *Passed by Congress July 6, 1965. Ratified February 10, 1967.*
Note: Article II, section 1, of the Constitution was affected by the Twenty-Fifth amendment

Section 4. Whenever the Vice President and a majority of either the principal officers of the executive departments or of such other body as Congress may by law provide, transmit to the President pro tempore of the Senate and the Speaker of the House of Representatives their written declaration that the President is unable to discharge the powers and duties of his office, the Vice President shall immediately assume the powers and duties of the office as Acting President.

Thereafter, when the President transmits to the President pro tempore of the Senate and the Speaker of the House of Representatives his written declaration that no inability exists, he shall resume the powers and duties of his office unless the Vice President and a majority of either the principal officers of the executive department or of such other body as Congress may by law provide, transmit within four days to the President pro tempore of the Senate and the Speaker of the House of Representatives their written declaration that the President is unable to discharge the powers and duties of his office. Thereupon Congress shall decide the issue, assembling within forty-eight hours for that purpose if not in session. If the Congress, within twenty-one days after receipt of the latter written declaration, or, if Congress is not in session, within twenty-one days after Congress is required to assemble, determines by two-thirds vote of both Houses that the President is unable to discharge the powers and duties of his office, the Vice President shall continue to discharge the same as Acting President; otherwise, the President shall resume the powers and duties of his office.

AMENDMENT XXVI.[19]

Section 1. The right of citizens of the United States, who are eighteen years of age or older, to vote shall not be denied or abridged by the United States or by any State on account of age.

Section 2. The Congress shall have power to enforce this article by appropriate legislation.

AMENDMENT XXVII.[20]

No law, varying the compensation for the services of the Senators and Representatives, shall take effect, until an election of Representatives shall have intervened.

19: *Passed by Congress March 23, 1971. Ratified July 1, 1971.*
Note: Amendment 14, section 2, of the Constitution was modified by section 1 of the Twenty-Sixth Amendment.

20: *Originally proposed Sept. 25, 1789. Ratified May 7, 1992.*

ACKNOWLEDGMENTS

Thanks to my assistant, Maura Kelly, who typed the drafts of my argument at all hours of the day, and to my son Elon and daughter Ella, who lovingly critiqued my speech and supported my controversial efforts. Thanks also to Jamin, Barbara, Lori, and Lyle, whose lives I made more difficult but whom I appreciate and love very much. And the greatest appreciation to Carolyn, who improves everything I do.